McGraw-Hill Reading WonderWorks INTERVENTION

Grade 3

Assessment

CCSS Assessing the Common Core State Standards

Mc Graw Hill Education

Bothell, WA • Chicago, IL • Columbus, OH • New York, NY

Cover: Nathan Love

www.mheonline.com/readingwonderworks

Mc Graw Hill Education

Copyright © McGraw-Hill Education

All rights reserved. The contents, or parts thereof, may be reproduced in print form for non-profit educational use with *McGraw-Hill Reading WonderWorks*, provided such reproductions bear copyright notice, but may not be reproduced in any form for any other purpose without the prior written consent of McGraw-Hill Education, including, but not limited to, network storage or transmission, or broadcast for distance learning.

Send all inquiries to:
McGraw-Hill Education
Two Penn Plaza
New York, New York 10121

ISBN: 978-0-02-129748-1
MHID: 0-02-129748-7

Printed in the United States of America.

4 5 6 7 8 9 RHR 18 17 16 15 14

TABLE OF CONTENTS

Teacher Introduction v

Weekly Assessment

Unit 1
Week 1 Assessment 10
Week 2 Assessment 12
Week 3 Assessment 14
Week 4 Assessment 16
Week 5 Assessment 18

Unit 2
Week 1 Assessment 20
Week 2 Assessment 22
Week 3 Assessment 24
Week 4 Assessment 26
Week 5 Assessment 28

Unit 3
Week 1 Assessment 30
Week 2 Assessment 32
Week 3 Assessment 34
Week 4 Assessment 36
Week 5 Assessment 38

Unit 4
Week 1 Assessment 40
Week 2 Assessment 42
Week 3 Assessment 44
Week 4 Assessment 46
Week 5 Assessment 48

Unit 5
Week 1 Assessment 50
Week 2 Assessment 52
Week 3 Assessment 54
Week 4 Assessment 56
Week 5 Assessment 58

Unit 6
Week 1 Assessment 60
Week 2 Assessment 62
Week 3 Assessment 64
Week 4 Assessment 66
Week 5 Assessment 68

Mid-Unit Assessment

Unit 1 Assessment 72
Unit 2 Assessment 80
Unit 3 Assessment 88
Unit 4 Assessment 96
Unit 5 Assessment 104
Unit 6 Assessment 112

Unit Assessment

Unit 1 Assessment 122
Unit 2 Assessment 131
Unit 3 Assessment 140
Unit 4 Assessment 149
Unit 5 Assessment 158
Unit 6 Assessment 167

Exit Assessment

Unit 1 Assessment 178
Unit 2 Assessment 187
Unit 3 Assessment 196
Unit 4 Assessment 205
Unit 5 Assessment 214
Unit 6 Assessment 223

TABLE OF CONTENTS

Oral Reading Fluency Assessment

Units 1–2 234   Units 3–4 250
                    Units 5–6 266

Scoring Sheets

Weekly Assessment 283   Unit Assessment 286
Mid-Unit Assessment 285   Exit Assessment 287

Answer Keys

Weekly Assessment 288   Unit Assessment 309
Mid-Unit Assessment 303   Exit Assessment 315

Assessment

The *Assessment* BLM is an integral part of the complete assessment program aligned with the Common Core State Standards (CCSS) and the core reading and intervention curriculums of **McGraw-Hill Reading WonderWorks** and **McGraw-Hill Reading Wonders**.

Purpose of *Assessment*

The instruction in **McGraw-Hill Reading WonderWorks** is parallel to the instruction in **McGraw-Hill Reading Wonders**. Student results in *Assessment* provide a picture of achievement within **McGraw-Hill Reading WonderWorks** and a signal as to whether students can successfully transition back to Approaching Level reading instruction.

Assessment offers the opportunity to monitor student progress in a steady and structured manner while providing formative assessment data.

As students complete each week of the intervention program, they will be assessed on their understanding of weekly vocabulary words and their ability to access and comprehend complex literary and informational selections using text evidence.

At the key 3-week and 6-week reporting junctures, assessments measure student understanding of previously-taught vocabulary words and comprehension skills and provide evidence of student progress through the curriculum. If students show a level of mastery at the end of a unit, an assessment to exit out of **McGraw-Hill Reading WonderWorks** and into the Approaching Level instruction of **McGraw-Hill Reading Wonders** is available.

Throughout the unit, oral reading fluency passages are available to measure student ability to read connected text fluently, accurately, and with a measure of prosody.

The results of the assessments provided in *Assessment* can be used to inform subsequent instruction and assist with grouping and leveling designations.

Components of *Assessment*

Assessment features the following tests:
- Weekly Assessment
- Mid-Unit Assessment
- Unit Assessment
- Exit Assessment
- Oral Reading Fluency Assessment

Assessment focuses on key areas of English Language Arts as identified by the CCSS—Reading, Language, and Fluency. To assess Reading and Language proficiency, students read selections and respond to items focusing on comprehension skills, vocabulary words, literary elements, and text features. These items assess the ability to access meaning from the text and demonstrate understanding of words and phrases. To assess Fluency, students read passages for one minute to measure their words correct per minute (WCPM) and accuracy rates.

Assessment • Teacher Introduction

Weekly Assessment

The Weekly Assessment features a "cold read" reading selection (informational or narrative based on the weekly reading focus) and 5 items—three items on the weekly comprehension skill and two items that ask students to show how context helps them identify the meaning of a vocabulary word. (For weeks in which poetry is the featured genre, vocabulary items are replaced by items assessing literary elements.) Students will provide text evidence to support their answers.

Administering Weekly Assessment

Each test should be administered once the instruction for the specific week is completed. Make a copy of the assessment and the Scoring Sheet for each student. The Scoring Sheet allows for informal comments on student responses and adds to an understanding of strengths and weaknesses.

After each student has a copy of the assessment, provide a version of the following directions: **Say:** *Write your name and the date on the question pages for this assessment.* (When students are finished, continue with the directions.) *You will read a selection and answer questions about it. Read the selection and the questions that follow it carefully. Write your responses on the lines provided. Go back to the text to underline and circle the text evidence that supports your answers. When you have completed the assessment, put your pencil down and turn the pages over. You may begin now.*

Answer procedural questions during the assessment, but do not provide any assistance on the items or selections. After the class has completed the assessment, ask students to verify that their names and the date are written on the necessary pages.

Alternatively, you may choose to work through the assessment with the students. This will provide an additional opportunity for you to observe their ability to access complex text in a more informal group setting.

Evaluating the Weekly Assessment

Each Weekly Assessment is worth 10 points, with each item worth 2 points. Use the scoring rubric below to assign a point total per item. A Weekly Answer Key is provided to help with scoring. Student results should provide a clear picture of their understanding of the weekly comprehension skill and the weekly vocabulary words. Reteach tested skills if assessment results point to a clear deficiency.

\	Weekly Assessment Scoring Rubric
Score	**Description**
2	• Reasonable, clear, and specific • Supported by accurate and relevant text evidence • Shows ability to access complex text
1	• Reasonable but somewhat unclear or vague • Supported by general, incomplete, partially accurate, or partially relevant text evidence • Shows some ability to access complex text
0	• Incorrect, unreasonable, or too vague to understand • Not supported by relevant text evidence • Shows no understanding of how to access complex text

Evidence may be specific words from the text or a paraphrase.

Mid-Unit Assessment

The Mid-Unit Assessment presents a snapshot of student understanding at the key 3-week instructional interval. This test features two "cold read" reading selections and 10 selected response items—seven items on the featured comprehension skills in Weeks 1–3 and three items that ask students to show how context helps them identify the meaning of a vocabulary word.

Administering Mid-Unit Assessment

Each test should be administered at the end of Week 3 instruction. Make a copy of the assessment and the Scoring Sheet for each student.

After each student has a copy of the assessment, provide a version of the following directions: **Say:** *Write your name and the date on the question pages for this assessment.* (When students are finished, continue with the directions.) *You will read two selections and answer questions about them. Read the selections and the questions that follow them carefully. Choose the correct answer to each question and completely fill in the bubble next to it. When you have completed the assessment, put your pencil down and turn the pages over. You may begin now.*

NOTE: The directions above can be used when students take the Unit and Exit Assessments.

Evaluating the Mid-Unit Assessment

Each Mid-Unit Assessment is worth 10 points, with each item worth 1 point. An Answer Key is provided to help with scoring. Note student success or difficulty with specific skills. Use this data to determine the instructional focus going forward. Reteach tested skills for students who score 5 points or less on the comprehension items and 2 points or less on the vocabulary items.

Unit and Exit Assessment

The Unit Assessment tests student mastery of the key instructional content featured in the unit. This test features two "cold read" reading selections (one narrative text and one informational text) and 15 selected response items—ten items on the unit's comprehension skills and five items that ask students to show how context helps them identify the meaning of a vocabulary word.

The Exit Assessment is a "parallel" test to the Unit Assessment. It assesses the same skills and pool of vocabulary words using the same format. The key differentiator between the tests is the higher level of text complexity featured in the reading selections, a level more in line with the rigor found in Approaching Level *McGraw-Hill Reading Wonders* materials.

Assessment • Teacher Introduction

Moving from Unit to Exit Assessment

Administer the Unit Assessment to ALL students at the close of unit instruction. Make a copy of the assessment and the Scoring Sheet for each student. Each Unit Assessment is worth 15 points, with each item worth 1 point. An Answer Key is provided to help with scoring.

If students score 13 or higher on the Unit Assessment, administer the Exit Assessment. The Exit Assessment is ONLY for those students who reach this Unit Assessment benchmark.

Oral Reading Fluency Assessment

Fluency passages are included to help assess the level at which students have progressed beyond decoding into comprehension. When readers can read the words in connected text automatically, they are free to focus on using the critical thinking skills essential to constructing meaning from complex text.

24 fiction and nonfiction passages are included to help you assess fluency. The passages are set in three Unit/Lexile bands—the first set of eight is for Units 1 and 2, the next set of eight is for Units 3 and 4, and the final set of eight is for Units 5 and 6.

See pages 6 and 7 of *Fluency Assessment* for directions on administering and scoring oral reading fluency passages and for the unit-specific benchmark WCPM scores.

Transitioning into *McGraw-Hill Reading Wonders* Instruction

Moving students into Approaching Level *McGraw-Hill Reading Wonders* instruction at the completion of a unit should be guided by assessment data, student performance during the unit instruction, and informal observation of student progress.

Use the following assessment criteria to help judge student readiness for Approaching Level designation and materials:

- Unit Assessment score of 13 or higher
- Ability to comprehend and analyze the Level Up Approaching Leveled Reader
- Score of 3 or higher on Level Up Write About Reading assignment
- Mastery of the unit benchmark skills in the Foundational Skills Kit and *Reading Wonders* Adaptive Learning
- WCPM score and accuracy rate that meet or exceed the unit goals
- Exit Assessment score of 13 or higher

Weekly Assessment

UNIT 1 WEEK 1 Name: _____ Date: _____

Read "Home Sweet Home" before you answer Numbers 1 through 5.

Home Sweet Home

Turtles live in their shells. They like it this way. They can sleep any place they like. They stop and rest in their shells.

Once there was a turtle named Tom. He was not happy or **satisfied**. Tom wanted more.

"I want a new place to call home," he said.

Tom stayed with Eagle. Eagle's nest was very high. It had a nice view. But Tom made a **discovery**. He felt scared in the high nest. Tom found out he was scared of heights.

Tom went to live with Bear. Bear's den was very nice. It was cool in summer. But winter came and Bear went to sleep. Tom had to go. He did not want to wake his sleeping friend.

Tom tried other homes. Beaver's lodge was noisy. Rabbit's hole was dark.

Tom stopped looking for a new home.

"I wanted a new place to call home," said Tom. "But in my shell, I am always at home."

GO ON →

Name: _____ Date: _____

Use "Home Sweet Home" to answer Numbers 1 through 5.

1 **Circle** the word that means almost the SAME as *satisfied*.

2 Tom wants more than other turtles. **Underline** the sentence that tells what Tom wants.

3 What *discovery* does Tom make?
_____
_____

Circle the clues that help you know what the word *discovery* means.

4 What does Tom like about Bear's den?
_____
_____

5 Why does Tom stop looking for a new home?
_____
_____

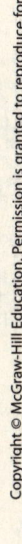

Weekly Assessment • Unit 1, Week 1

UNIT 1 WEEK 2 Name: _____ Date: _____

Read "The Red Bracelet" before you answer Numbers 1 through 5.

The Red Bracelet

It was a big day in the Chen house. Joy's little brother turned one month old today. Family and friends had come to **celebrate**. Everyone was having a good time. Some brought red eggs. Others brought red envelopes. Giving gifts on this day was a Chinese **tradition**. It was an important custom.

Joy sat on the couch. She felt sad. Aunt Lin sat down beside her.

"What is wrong?" asked Aunt Lin.

"I do not have a gift," said Joy.

Then Aunt Lin had an idea. She took Joy into the kitchen. There were scraps of red paper all around.

"We can make something for him!" said Aunt Lin.

They sat down and got started. Soon the gift was finished! Joy gave Aunt Lin a hug.

Joy went over to her brother. She held a red paper bracelet. She put it on his wrist.

"What a good gift!" said her mother. "What a good sister!"

Joy smiled. She felt happy again.

GO ON →

Name: _____ Date: _____

Use "The Red Bracelet" to answer Numbers 1 through 5.

1 Why is Joy sad at the BEGINNING of the story?

_____

_____

Underline the details that support your answer.

2 **Circle** the words that help you figure out what *celebrate* means.

3 Joy gives Aunt Lin a hug for helping her. What happens next?

_____

_____

Draw a box around the sentences that support your answer.

4 **Circle** the words that mean almost the SAME as *tradition*.

5 How does Joy feel at the END of the story?

_____

Underline the text evidence.

Weekly Assessment • Unit 1, Week 2

UNIT 1 WEEK 3 Name: _____ Date: _____

Read "A Big Party" before you answer Numbers 1 through 5.

A Big Party

Waiting for Sofia

I waited for Sofia after school. Sofia is more than a **classmate**. She is my best friend. I invited her to my house. But she could not come.

"I'm sorry, Kate," Sofia said. "I have too much to do today. First, I have to do homework. Next, I have a piano lesson. Last, I have to help get ready for my sister's party."

A "Growing Up" Party

"What kind of party is it?" I asked.

"It is a big party," Sofia explained. "It happens when a girl turns fifteen. It means she is growing up. I want to **contribute** to the party. I am helping set up the hall. There will be two hundred guests."

"That is a lot!" I said.

"Yes," Sofia said. "But it is a special day. Our family and friends will be there. I can come over next week after the party."

"I will let you get to work, then!" I said.

GO ON →

Name: _____   Date: _____

Use "A Big Party" to answer Numbers 1 through 5.

1 **Circle** the word that helps to show what *classmate* means.

What is a *classmate*?
_____
_____

2 What must Sofia do FIRST in the section "Waiting for Sofia"?
_____
_____
_____

Underline the next thing Sofia has to do.

3 What is the LAST thing Sofia has to do?
_____
_____
_____

Draw a box around the signal word.

4 **Circle** how Sofia will *contribute* to her sister's party.

What does *contribute* mean?
_____
_____

5 What will Sofia do AFTER the party?
_____
_____

STOP

Weekly Assessment • Unit 1, Week 3   Grade 3   15

UNIT 1, WEEK 4

Name: _____ Date: _____

Read "Ann's Good Idea" before you answer Numbers 1 through 5.

Ann's Good Idea

Ann Moore was a nurse. She worked in Africa. She saw mothers carry their babies on their backs. They put the babies in slings, or loops of cloth. The babies stayed close to their mothers. As a result, they felt safe. They stayed calm.

Ann came home. She had a baby. She wrapped her baby in a blanket. Then she tied the blanket to her back. But the baby kept slipping. This was a big problem. Ann had to find a **solution**.

She had an idea for a new type of sling. It looked like a backpack. It had two straps. It also had an open pouch, or pocket, to hold the baby in place.

Ann's sling made life better for parents. It was **simple**, or easy, to use. Parents could carry their babies around with them. They could keep their arms free for other things. Because of this, they could cook or work. They could even ride bikes. What a good idea!

GO ON →

Weekly Assessment • Unit 1, Week 4

Name: _____ Date: _____

Use "Ann's Good Idea" to answer Numbers 1 through 5.

1 Why did the babies in Africa feel safe?

_____

_____

Underline the signal words.

2 What happened when Ann wrapped her baby in a blanket?

_____

Underline the sentence that tells what happened.

3 **Circle** the word that means the OPPOSITE of *solution*.

What does *solution* mean?

_____

4 **Draw a box** around the text evidence that tells why Ann's sling was a good idea.

5 **Circle** a word that means almost the SAME as *simple*.

Weekly Assessment • Unit 1, Week 4   Grade 3

Read "Muir Woods National Monument" before you answer Numbers 1 through 5.

Muir Woods National Monument

Redwoods are **massive** trees. They can be almost 400 feet tall. Long ago, redwoods grew all over California. Then the gold miners came. They needed wood. They cut down many redwoods. People began to worry. They did not want to lose these trees.

William Kent wanted to help. He bought a redwood forest in 1905. Then he gave the forest to the country. He asked the president to make it a national **monument**. He wanted to keep the forest safe for people to enjoy.

The president liked this gift. He wanted to name it for William Kent. But Kent thought it should be named for John Muir. Muir wrote about California. He wanted to protect nature. His work made other people want to help.

On January 9, 1908, the president created the Muir Woods National Monument. People still go there today. They go to see the redwoods. They remember John Muir. They enjoy the nature he loved.

GO ON →

Name: _____ Date: _____

Use "Muir Woods National Monument" to answer Numbers 1 through 5.

1 **Circle** the words that help to show that redwood trees are *massive*.

2 **Underline** key details that tell why William Kent bought a redwood forest.

3 **Circle** the words that help you figure out what *monument* means.

What is a *monument*?
_____
_____

4 **Underline** the date when Muir Woods became a national monument.

Why do people still visit it today?
_____
_____

5 What is the MAIN idea of the passage?
_____
_____

Draw a box around key details that tell about the MAIN idea.

Weekly Assessment • Unit 1, Week 5   Grade 3

Read "Cat and Fish" before you answer Numbers 1 through 5.

Cat and Fish

A long time ago, Cat loved water. She sailed her boat up and down the river.

Fish was Cat's friend. Fish told Cat not to sail out to sea.

"The waves are too big," Fish said. "Your boat is too small. It will tip over."

But Cat wanted to **attempt** it. She had to try to sail out to sea. So Cat sailed her little boat down the river. She sailed all the way to the sea.

The wind was strong and the waves were big. Cat's boat rocked back and forth. It was going to tip over!

Fish swam up next to Cat. "I will help you," he said.

Fish turned Cat's boat around. He pulled the boat back to the river where it was safe.

After that day, Cat did not like water. She became shy and **timid** around it. Cat should have listened to her friend. Fish knew more about the sea than anyone.

GO ON →

Name: _____ Date: _____

Use "Cat and Fish" to answer Numbers 1 through 5.

1 Why does Fish think Cat should not sail out to sea?

_____

_____

2 **Circle** a word that means almost the SAME as *attempt*.

3 Why does Cat need help at sea?

_____

_____

Underline how Fish helps Cat.

4 **Circle** the word that means almost the SAME as *timid*.

When does Cat become *timid* around water?

_____

5 What is the theme or message of this story?

_____

_____

Draw a box around the text evidence at the END of the story.

Weekly Assessment • Unit 2, Week 1   Grade 3   21

UNIT 2 WEEK 2 Name: _____ Date: _____

Read "Tom Moves to America" before you answer Numbers 1 through 5.

Tom Moves to America

In 1875, America was a young country. It was also growing. People moved into cities. They moved west to farm. Many came from other countries. Tom's family **immigrated** to America from Norway. This is a country in Europe.

Mom and Dad wanted a farm in America. Tom did not want to go.

"I will miss my friends," he said.

"You will make new friends," Dad said. "You can find friends anywhere you go."

They all left by boat and **arrived** after days of sailing. Then they traveled west by train. Their farm was near a small town. Mom and Dad were happy. This made Tom happy. But Tom had to start school. It would be hard without his friends.

Tom did not have to worry. There were many new kids at the school. The kids talked about where they came from. They talked about their new home.

"Dad was right," Tom thought. "You can find friends anywhere you go."

GO ON →

Name: _____ Date: _____

Use "Tom Moves to America" to answer Numbers 1 through 5.

1 **Circle** the words that help you figure out what *immigrated* means.

2 Why doesn't Tom want to move to America?
_____
_____

Underline the sentence that shows how he feels.

3 **Circle** the word that means the OPPOSITE of *arrived*.

What does *arrived* mean?
_____
_____

4 Tom thinks it will be hard to start school without his old friends. **Underline** why this is not true.

5 What does Tom learn in the story?
_____
_____

Draw a box around the text evidence.

STOP

Weekly Assessment • Unit 2, Week 2 — Grade 3 — 23

UNIT 2 WEEK 3 Name: _____ Date: _____

Read "The United States Government" before you answer Numbers 1 through 5.

The United States Government

The U.S. **government** rules our country. There are three parts, or branches. Each branch is important.

The president leads one branch. The president has important powers. One power is to keep our country safe. Another is to make sure we follow our laws.

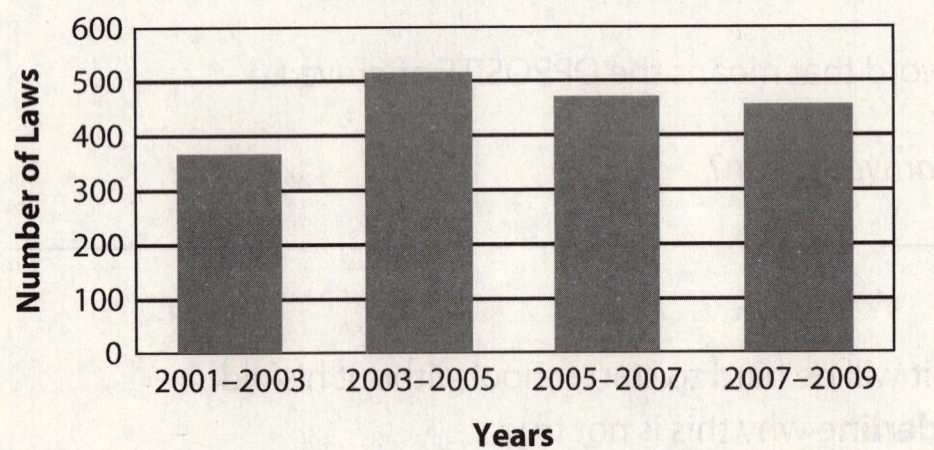

Laws Signed by President

Years	Number of Laws
2001–2003	~370
2003–2005	~520
2005–2007	~475
2007–2009	~460

The president helps to create many laws.

Congress is a group that leads the second branch. It makes laws for our country. We need laws.

The Supreme Court leads the third branch. It makes important **decisions** about laws. It chooses if a law is right or wrong for our country.

The branches have different powers. No branch has too much power. Our government works well this way.

GO ON →

Name: _____ Date: _____

Use "The United States Government" to answer Numbers 1 through 5.

1 **Circle** what our *government* does.

2 **Underline** the sentence that tells what the author thinks about the branches of government.

3 **Draw a box** around the title of the bar graph.

How does the graph support the author's point of view that the president's powers are important?

_____

_____

4 **Circle** the word that helps you understand what *decisions* means.

5 Why does the author think our government works well?

_____

_____

Underline the details that support your answer.

Weekly Assessment • Unit 2, Week 3 — Grade 3

UNIT 2 WEEK 4   Name: _____   Date: _____

Read "Saving California's Sea Otter" before you answer Numbers 1 through 5.

Saving California's Sea Otter

Sea otters live in California. It is fun to watch them. They swim on their backs and play. Once there were many otters. Now the **population**, or number, is small. This is sad. But some people are working to help.

An aquarium helps sea animals. The workers are **caretakers**. They take good care of sea otters. They help sick and hurt otters. They also save babies that are lost. They use grown otters to teach pups. The pups learn to take care of themselves. Then they go back to the sea.

Aquariums want sea otters to live safely. The workers help to increase the number of otters in nature.

Sea Otters in North America

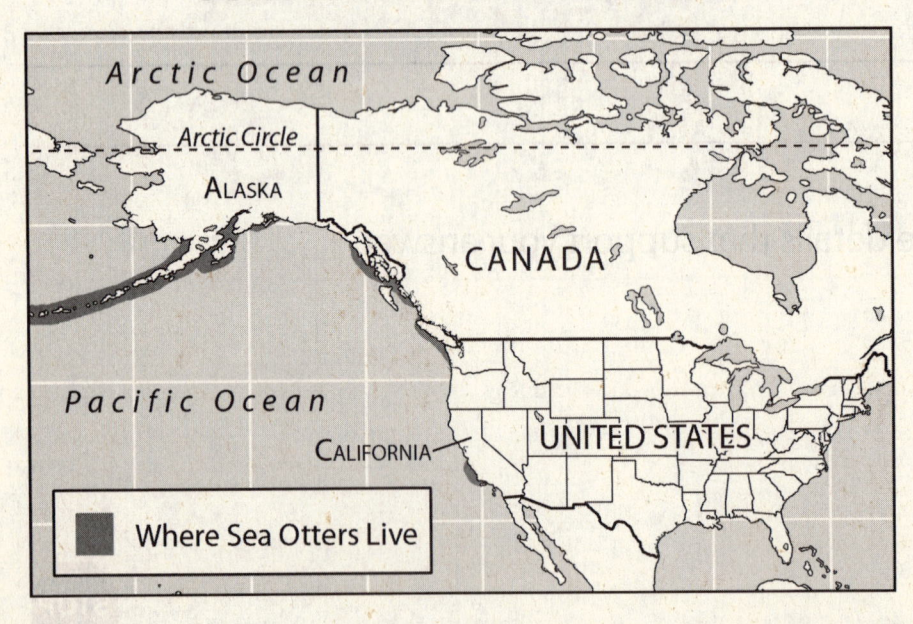

[Map showing Arctic Ocean, Arctic Circle, Alaska, Canada, Pacific Ocean, California, United States, with legend: Where Sea Otters Live]

GO ON →

Name: _____ Date: _____

Use "Saving California's Sea Otter" to answer Numbers 1 through 5.

1 **Underline** the word that tells what the author thinks about watching otters.

2 **Circle** the word that helps you know what *population* means.

3 **Circle** the words that tell what *caretakers* do.

How do aquarium workers act like *caretakers* to otters?
_____
_____

4 What does the author think about what aquariums do?
_____
_____

Underline a detail that shows a result of their work.

5 **Draw a box** around the title of the map.

Why did the author include the map about sea otters?
_____
_____

Weekly Assessment • Unit 2, Week 4   Grade 3   27

Read "The Fish and the Whale" before you answer Numbers 1 through 5.

The Fish and the Whale

An observer who stood on the shore

Saw a sight she had not seen before.

   In a boat with a sail

   Were a fish and a whale

Wearing clothes that they bought at a store.

The whale wore a large dress that was white,

And the fish had a hat—what a sight!

   They started to giggle

   And bounce with a wiggle.

The observer just laughed in delight!

GO ON →

Name: _____ Date: _____

Use "The Fish and the Whale" to answer Numbers 1 through 5.

① How can you tell that this funny poem is a limerick?
_____
_____

② **Underline** the words in the first stanza that rhyme with *shore*.

Write another word from the poem that rhymes with *shore*.
_____

③ **Draw a box** around the words that start with the same sound in the first line of the last stanza.

What is this called?
_____

④ **Circle** text evidence that shows what the poet thinks about the events in the poem.

⑤ What is the poet's point of view?
_____
_____

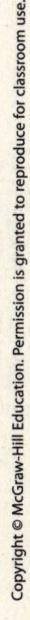

Weekly Assessment · Unit 2, Week 5   Grade 3

Read "The Trade" before you answer Numbers 1 through 5.

The Trade

Fox and Deer sat by the river. They were not happy at all. They did not like the way they were made.

"I do not like being so short," said Fox. "It would be wonderful if I were tall. Then I could run like the wind. Wouldn't that be **fabulous**?"

"I do not like being so tall," said Deer. "I wish I were short so that I could hide in the ground."

Fox and Deer decided to trade legs. Now Fox had long legs and could run very fast. Deer had short legs and could hide easily.

But Fox could no longer hunt under the ground. She got hungry. Deer could no longer reach the leaves in the trees. He got hungry, too.

"I think we made a mistake," said Fox. "Our legs are different and **unique**. They helped us in their own ways."

Fox and Deer decided to trade again. They were happy to have their own legs back.

Name: _____ Date: _____

Use "The Trade" to answer Numbers 1 through 5.

1 **Underline** Fox and Deer's problem at the BEGINNING of the story.

2 **Circle** the word that means almost the SAME as *fabulous*.

What does Fox think would be *fabulous*?
_____
_____

3 How do Fox and Deer try to solve their problem?
_____

Underline the text evidence.

4 **Circle** the word that helps you figure out what *unique* means.

How are Fox and Deer's legs *unique*?
_____

5 **Draw a box** around the sentence that tells the solution at the END of the story.

STOP

Weekly Assessment • Unit 3, Week 1 — Grade 3

UNIT 3 WEEK 2   Name: _____   Date: _____

Read "Yellowstone National Park" before you answer Numbers 1 through 5.

Yellowstone National Park

It was 1947. Tim's family was visiting Yellowstone National Park. Dave was their tour guide. He pointed out some bison. Tim did not listen because he was thinking of his friends at home.

"There used to be a lot more bison here," Dave said. "People thought they would **disappear** and never be seen again. The park keeps them safe."

"That's interesting. I didn't know that," Tim said.

Dave thought he knew another thing that would interest Tim. So he showed the family a geyser. At first, Tim heard a rumbling noise. Then, a huge stream of water shot up from the ground! Tim looked at the geyser in **amazement**. He was surprised the water could shoot so high!

"President Teddy Roosevelt visited Yellowstone," Dave said. "He loved nature and wanted to keep it safe. As a result, he helped pass laws to set up more national parks," said Dave.

"I agree with the president," said Tim. "National parks are great!"

GO ON →

Name: _____ Date: _____

Use "Yellowstone National Park" to answer Numbers 1 through 5.

1 Why doesn't Tim listen to Dave at the BEGINNING of the story?

_____

Underline the cause.

2 **Circle** the words that help you figure out what *disappear* means.

What is the meaning of *disappear*?

_____

3 Why does Dave show Tim the geyser?

_____

4 **Circle** the word that helps you figure out what *amazement* means.

5 Why did Teddy Roosevelt help set up more national parks?

_____

Draw a box around the signal words.

STOP

Weekly Assessment • Unit 3, Week 2   Grade 3   33

UNIT 3 WEEK 3 Name: _____ Date: _____

Read "Objects in Our Solar System" before you answer Numbers 1 through 5.

Objects in Our Solar System

Have you ever studied the night sky? We have always been curious about **astronomy**. Long ago, people thought that everything in space moved around Earth. Then they learned that all planets move around the Sun.

The Sun and planets are not the only objects, or things, in our **solar system**. There are also moons and asteroids (AS-ter-oyds). A moon moves around a planet. We have already found many moons. There are probably more. Some are larger than Earth's moon. Others are quite small.

Asteroids are chunks of rock. Some are many miles wide. Others are just a few feet wide. They move around the Sun and between the planets.

There are even more objects in our solar system. We continue to learn about space every day.

Space Objects

Objects	Movement	How Many
Planet	around the Sun	8
Moon	around a planet	more than 146
Asteroid	around the Sun	more than 90,000

GO ON →

Name: _____ Date: _____

Use "Objects in Our Solar System" to answer Numbers 1 through 5.

1 **Circle** the words that help you figure out what *astronomy* means.

What do you see when you study *astronomy*?
_____

2 What does a moon move around?
_____

Underline the key detail that tells how a moon moves.

3 **Circle** the clues that help you know what a *solar system* is.

4 Read the chart. Tell how many asteroids there are in our solar system.
_____

Draw a box around the number of planets in our solar system.

5 What is the MAIN idea of this article?
_____
_____

STOP

Weekly Assessment • Unit 3, Week 3   Grade 3

Read "Deer Antlers" before you answer Numbers 1 through 5.

Deer Antlers

Antlers are made of bone. They grow on top of the head of a male deer, or buck. You may think all antlers look **similar**. But their shapes can be quite different.

Bucks sometimes fight each other with their antlers. The antlers crash. They push against each other. Antlers must be tough not to break.

Antlers grow with a soft covering. This comes off before bucks are ready to fight. Then the antlers become dry. People have looked closely at antlers. They have **observed** how antlers get strong when they are dry.

Usually, things break more easily when they are dry. People want to figure out why antlers are different. This will help them create things as strong as antlers.

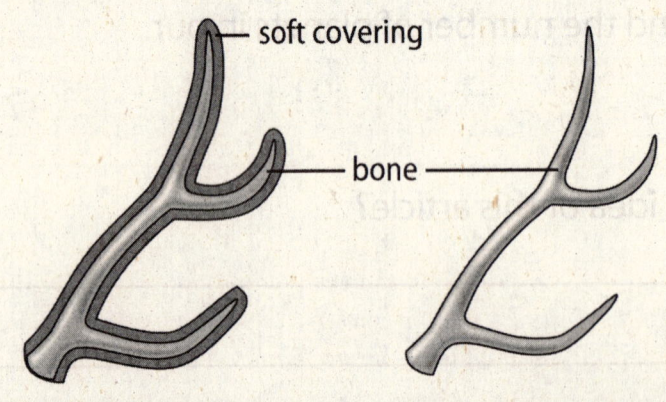

soft covering
bone

Antler with soft covering   **Antler after it dries**

GO ON →

Name: _____ Date: _____

Use "Deer Antlers" to answer Numbers 1 through 5.

1 What are deer antlers?
_____

Underline two details that tell what deer antlers are.

2 **Circle** the word that means the OPPOSITE of *similar*.

What does *similar* mean?
_____

3 Look at the diagram. What does it show?
_____
_____

4 **Circle** the words that tell you what *observed* means.

5 What is the MAIN idea of "Deer Antlers"?
_____

Draw a box around the key details that support this idea.

Weekly Assessment • Unit 3, Week 4   Grade 3   37

UNIT 3 WEEK 5 Name: _____ Date: _____

Read "The Vikings" before you answer Numbers 1 through 5.

The Vikings

Many years ago, the Vikings left their home. They went to live in new lands. As part of their **emigration**, they went to Iceland and Greenland.

One story says the Vikings then traveled west from Greenland. They found a new land. First, they explored the land. Next, they built a small town. Finally, they fought with the natives there. They decided to leave.

Some people thought the Vikings had reached North America. In 1960, a man went to Canada to find out. First, he found bits of old Viking houses. Then, he found Viking tools. This proved that the Vikings were the first settlers in Canada. These brave **pioneers** reached North America 500 years before Christopher Columbus!

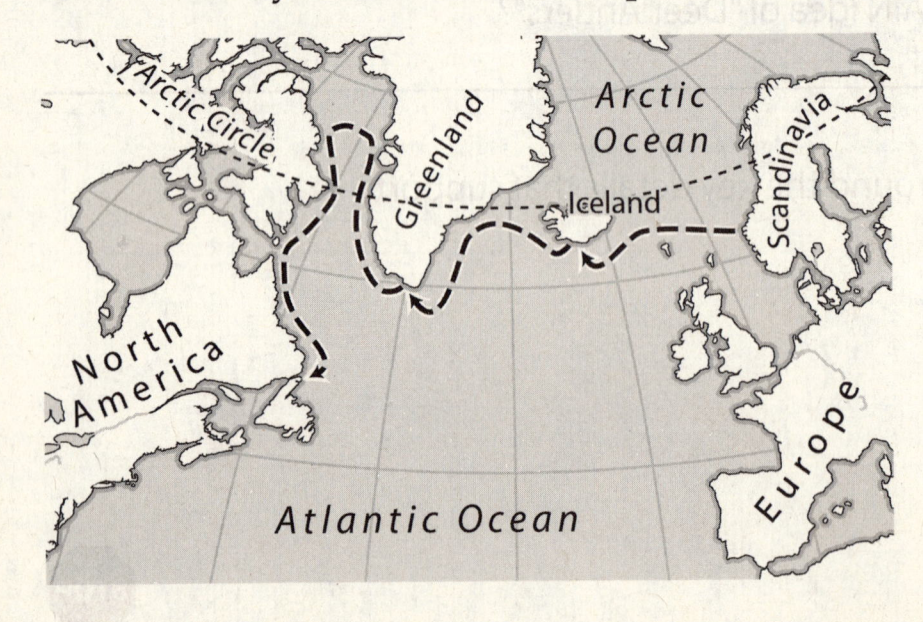

GO ON →

Name: _____ Date: _____

Use "The Vikings" to answer Numbers 1 through 5.

1 **Underline** the words that help you understand what *emigration* means.

2 What did the Vikings do right BEFORE they left the new land they found?

_____

Circle the word that tells time order for this event.

3 In 1960, what did the man in Canada find FIRST?

_____

Circle what he found NEXT.

4 Which words help you understand the meaning of *pioneers*?

_____

5 Look at the map. Where did the Vikings begin their journey?

_____

Draw a box around the place on the map where their journey ended.

Weekly Assessment • Unit 3, Week 5   Grade 3

UNIT 4 WEEK 1

Read "The Loyal Parrot" before you answer Numbers 1 through 5.

The Loyal Parrot

There was a parrot who lived in my fruit tree. He loved the tree very much. He loved smelling the **aroma** of the tree's flowers. He loved eating its sweet fruit. He loved listening to the wind in its leaves.

"This tree has given me so much," the parrot said happily. "I will never live in another."

I heard the parrot's words. "Is the parrot telling the truth?" I wondered. "I will see if he is really loyal." So I stopped watering my fruit tree. It dried up its leaves, dropped off its flowers, and grew no more fruit.

"This tree has given me so much," the parrot said again. "I cannot leave when it is sick!" So the parrot stayed. He no longer smelled the tree's flowers. He no longer tasted its sweet fruit.

"I did not **expect** the parrot to stay!" I thought. "I was sure he would fly away and find another tree. He truly is a loyal friend!"

I watered the tree again. It grew back its leaves, flowers, and fruit. The parrot looked happy to have his old friend back.

GO ON →

Name: _____ Date: _____

Use "The Loyal Parrot" to answer Numbers 1 through 5.

1 **Circle** the word that helps you understand what *aroma* means.

What is the meaning of *aroma*?
_____

2 **Underline** details that tell what the narrator wonders about the parrot at the BEGINNING of the story.

What does the narrator decide to do?
_____
_____

3 **Circle** clues that tell what *expect* means.

4 What does the narrator think about the parrot's actions in the story?
_____
_____

5 How does the narrator MOST LIKELY feel about the parrot at the end of the story? Why?
_____
_____

Weekly Assessment • Unit 4, Week 1

Read "A Team of Twin Brothers" before you answer Numbers 1 through 5.

A Team of Twin Brothers

My name is Paul. My twin brother is John. We may look alike, but we have different **talents**, or things that we are good at. John is very good at playing sports. I think he is the best baseball player in our class. But playing music is easier for me than playing sports.

During baseball season, John gave me helpful tips. "Watch the ball closely," he told me. We practiced each afternoon. I began to catch more balls. With my brother's help, I think I was hitting the ball well, too.

In music class, we learned to play a song on a recorder. It is an instrument like a flute. We practiced the song for a school concert. I thought the recorder was easy to learn, but John could not figure out how to play it.

"Pay **attention** to my fingers," I said. John closely watched me play. Then he did the same thing with his fingers. After a while, he learned the song. John played it perfectly in the concert!

John and I do different things well. I think this makes us a good team.

GO ON →

Name: _____ Date: _____

Use "A Team of Twin Brothers" to answer Numbers 1 through 5.

1 **Circle** the words that help you figure out what *talents* means.

What are *talents*?
_____

2 **Underline** the details that show what Paul thinks about playing sports.

3 How does Paul's point of view about baseball change?
_____
_____

4 **Circle** the words that show what it means to pay *attention*.

5 Why does Paul think that he and his brother make a good team?
_____
_____

Draw a box around the details.

Weekly Assessment • Unit 4, Week 2   Grade 3   43

UNIT 4 WEEK 3 Name: _____ Date: _____

Read "Turtles and Tortoises" before you answer Numbers 1 through 5.

Turtles and Tortoises

Turtles and tortoises are a lot alike. Both use their hard shells for **protection**. The shells keep them safe from animals that hunt them. Both animals can also go underground for **shelter**. They dig holes in the ground to cover themselves from the heat or cold.

Turtles and tortoises are different, too. Turtles live mostly in water. They have webbed feet or long feet they use like flippers. Their feet help them swim.

Tortoises live on land. They do not have feet that help them in the water. Instead, they use their feet for walking. Their legs and feet look like stumps.

Turtles and tortoises have similar shells and act alike sometimes. But turtles live mostly in the water and tortoises live on land.

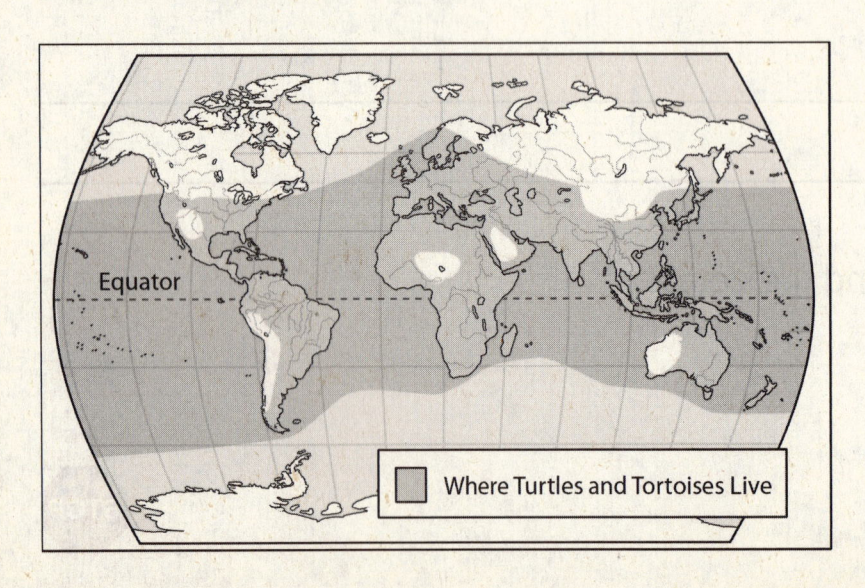

Equator

Where Turtles and Tortoises Live

GO ON →

Name: _____ Date: _____

Use "Turtles and Tortoises" to answer Numbers 1 through 5.

1 What do turtles and tortoises have that make them ALIKE?

_____

Circle the signal word that shows they are the SAME.

2 **Underline** the words that help you figure out what *protection* means.

Write the meaning of *protection*.

_____

3 How are tortoise feet and turtle feet DIFFERENT?

_____
_____

4 **Underline** how a tortoise and a turtle find *shelter*.

What does *shelter* mean?

_____

5 **Circle** a place on the map where turtles can be found but tortoises cannot. Use the information in the article to help you.

Weekly Assessment • Unit 4, Week 3

Read "Not Just an Artist" before you answer Numbers 1 through 5.

Not Just an Artist

Many people think the Wright brothers were the first people to fly. This is not true. People have studied **flight** for hundreds of years. Because of this, the Wright brothers learned what worked and what did not.

Leonardo Da Vinci lived in the 1400s. He was a famous artist and inventor. He was interested in flying. So, he studied the way that bats and birds flew. Da Vinci may not have built a flying machine, but he left his notes and drawings behind.

Da Vinci knew that *lift* was an important part of flying. Lift happens when wind goes over and under a wing. This allows birds to take off. Birds also use *thrust* to fly. They flap their wings to create thrust. Many of Da Vinci's drawings used this idea. Because we are heavier than birds, we could never fly by flapping wings. It would be **impossible**.

Today, we know that flight is about more than thrust and lift. But Da Vinci's notes helped to create the airplanes we use today.

Name: _____ Date: _____

Use "Not Just an Artist" to answer Numbers 1 through 5.

1 Write the words that help you know what *flight* means.
_____
_____

2 What helped the Wright brothers fly?
_____
_____

Circle the signal words.

3 **Draw a box** around the reason why Da Vinci studied bats and birds.

What signal word helped you find the answer?
_____
_____

4 Why do birds flap their wings?
_____
_____

5 **Underline** the words that help you figure out what *impossible* means.

What does *impossible* mean?
_____
_____

STOP

Weekly Assessment • Unit 4, Week 4   Grade 3   47

UNIT 4 WEEK 5   Name: _____   Date: _____

Read "Little Flower" before you answer Numbers 1 through 5.

Little Flower

Oh, little flower that brightens the woods.

Do you think it is odd or weird

That a single flower on a cold, dark path

Brings joy where once I feared?

You show that a great power,

May be found in the smallest flower.

Oh, little flower, you have a talent,

An extremely good gift of light.

Let me bring you water to help you grow,

So all the world may smile at your sight.

Grow, grow, oh little flower

For all the world to see.

Grow, grow, oh little flower.

And light the path for me.

GO ON →

Name: _____   Date: _____

Use "Little Flower" to answer Numbers 1 through 5.

1 How can you tell that this poem is free verse?
_____
_____

2 **Draw a box** around the second stanza.

Tell what the speaker means here.
_____
_____

3 **Underline** the words that rhyme in the third stanza.

4 Which word repeats in the fourth stanza?
_____

5 How does the speaker feel about the little flower?
_____
_____

Weekly Assessment • Unit 4, Week 5

UNIT 5 WEEK 1   Name: _____   Date: _____

Read the "The Golden Goose" before you answer Numbers 1 through 5.

The Golden Goose

Once upon a time, there lived two strong brothers. Their family was not wealthy and could not afford wood. Their mother asked the older brother to go into the forest and chop some. As the brother was walking, a thin, gray-haired man came up to him.

"Please," said the man in a gentle, **humble** voice. "I am very hungry. Do you have a piece of bread?"

The older brother had bread, but he did not want to give it away. So, he told the old man to go away. The brother took a step and tripped. Somehow his shoes had become tied together! He limped home without wood.

The younger brother was sent into the forest. The same man begged him for bread. This brother felt bad for him and gave his lunch away for free.

"Thank you! If you chop this tree down, you will find **payment** for your kindness."

The younger brother did just that. Inside the tree, he found a goose with feathers made of pure gold. Now his family could afford wood and more!

GO ON →

Name: _____ Date: _____

Use "The Golden Goose" to answer Numbers 1 through 5.

1 **Circle** the word that helps you figure out what *humble* means.

How does the man act in a *humble* way?

_____

2 **Underline** details that show what the older brother thinks about the man he meets in the forest.

3 What does the younger brother think about the man?

_____

_____

Draw a box around the text evidence.

4 **Circle** what the man gives the younger brother as *payment* for his kindness.

What does *payment* mean?

_____

5 What does the younger brother think about his gift?

_____

_____

Underline details that support your idea.

Weekly Assessment • Unit 5, Week 1   Grade 3   51

Read "Homemade Treasure" before you answer Numbers 1 through 5.

Homemade Treasure

"Oh, no!" Mark said in **frustration**. He was upset because it was raining and he could not play outside.

"Let's play inside," Tina said. "We can pretend we are pirates." Tina knew her brother loved pirates.

Mark thought the most important thing pirates needed was a treasure map. They found newspaper that had turned yellow and looked just like an old map!

"We need a telescope to look for treasure," Tina said. They used an empty roll of paper towels to make one.

Next, Mom helped them turn a used cardboard box into a treasure chest. Then she gave the kids old scarves to wear on their heads. "You look just like pirates," Mom said.

To make the treasure, they cut circles from cardboard. Then they wrapped the circles in used tinfoil. "Silver coins!" Tina said in a **jubilant** voice. She was very happy that it looked so good.

The kids played pirates all day. They thought it had been just as much fun making what they needed as it was to actually play.

GO ON →

Name: _____ Date: _____

Use "Homemade Treasure" to answer Numbers 1 through 5.

❶ Circle the details that tell why Mark feels *frustration*.

What does *frustration* mean?
_____

❷ Underline why Tina thinks her brother would like to play pirates.

❸ What does Mark think is important when playing pirates?
_____
_____

Underline the sentence that tells what he thinks.

❹ Circle the words that show what *jubilant* means.

❺ What do the kids think about making things to play pirates?
_____
_____

Draw a box around the text evidence.

Weekly Assessment • Unit 5, Week 2   Grade 3

UNIT 5 WEEK 3   Name: _____   Date: _____

Read "TV News Team" before you answer Numbers 1 through 5.

TV News Team

People watch the news to learn about events in their community. A news team must **respond**, or react, quickly to events to report the latest news. Reporting the news on TV takes amazing teamwork.

Reporters   Reporters go to where the event takes place. They find out more about it. They report what happened.

Camera People   Camera people film members of the news team. They choose the right camera **equipment** to use. These tools help them do their job. They use their cameras to "shoot" the story.

News Anchors   News anchors are like the hosts of the news program. They read the news on TV. They also ask reporters questions about their stories.

News Editors   News editors write for the anchors. They may also help reporters find out more about a story. They make sure that the information is true.

It takes a lot of teamwork to report the news on TV. But it is exciting work!

GO ON →

Name: _____ Date: _____

Use "TV News Team" to answer Numbers 1 through 5.

1 **Underline** the sentence that tells why people watch the news.

Explain why the author probably thinks the news is important.

_____

_____

2 What does a news team do when it *responds* to events?

_____

3 **Draw a box** around the sentence that shows what the author thinks about reporting the news on TV.

4 **Circle** the word that means almost the SAME as *equipment*.

5 Find the section "News Anchors." What does the author think about news anchors?

_____

_____

Underline the detail that tells what the author thinks.

Weekly Assessment • Unit 5, Week 3   Grade 3   **55**

Read "Eleanor Roosevelt" before you answer Numbers 1 through 5.

Eleanor Roosevelt

Eleanor Roosevelt was born in New York in 1884. As a girl, she traveled and saw many poor places. The people lived hard lives while others lived in comfort. This **unfairness** upset Eleanor, and she wanted to help.

Eleanor returned to New York City in 1902. There, she became a teacher. She helped workers live better, healthier lives. She also reported unsafe workplaces. Her work pushed the owners to make these places safer.

In 1905, Eleanor married Franklin Roosevelt. He later became President. As First Lady, Eleanor **continued** working to improve people's lives. She did many more things to help others and make our country a better place.

Dates in Eleanor's Life

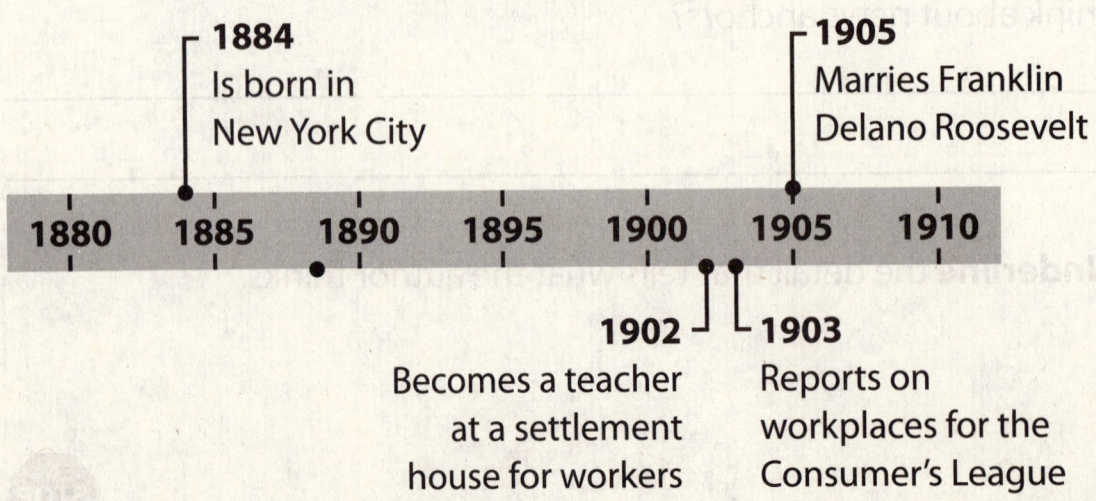

1884 Is born in New York City

1902 Becomes a teacher at a settlement house for workers

1903 Reports on workplaces for the Consumer's League

1905 Marries Franklin Delano Roosevelt

GO ON →

Name: _____ Date: _____

Use "Eleanor Roosevelt" to answer Numbers 1 through 5.

1 **Draw a box** around the sentence that tells about the *unfairness* that Eleanor saw in her travels.

What does *unfairness* mean?
_____

2 How did Eleanor work to make life better in New York City?
_____
_____

3 **Draw a box** around the clues that help you understand what *continued* means.

4 Look at the time line. **Circle** events that show Eleanor wanted to help others.

5 What is the author's point of view about Eleanor?
_____
_____

Underline the sentences that support your answer.

Weekly Assessment • Unit 5, Week 4 — Grade 3 — 57

UNIT 5 WEEK 5 Name: _____ Date: _____

Read "The Power of the Wind" before you answer Numbers 1 through 5.

The Power of the Wind

Wind has been used as an **energy** source for a long time. Sailboats used the power of wind to travel the Nile River long ago. But there are other ways to use wind.

Have you ever seen a windmill? These machines have been around for hundreds of years. A simple windmill has three blades that sit on top of a tall pole.

When the wind blows, the blades catch the wind. This causes them to turn. They use that wind power to complete a task. Early windmills were used to make grain into flour. They also pumped water. Today, windmills are used to create electricity.

Wind energy is good for a few reasons. It is **renewable**. This means it will not run out. It does not pollute the earth, either, like coal or oil does. As a result, many people think it is a great idea to use wind energy.

Energy Source	Effect on Our Planet
Wind	Does not pollute our planet
Coal and Oil	Does pollute our planet
Sun	Does not pollute our planet

GO ON →

Name: _____ Date: _____

Use "The Power of the Wind" to answer Numbers 1 through 5.

1 **Circle** the word that means almost the SAME as *energy*.

What does *energy* mean?
_____

2 What happens when windmill blades "catch" the wind?
_____

Underline the signal word.

3 **Circle** the words that explain what *renewable* means.

4 Why do many people think wind power is a great idea?
_____
_____

Draw a box around the signal words.

5 Look at the chart. Which energy source has a bad effect on the planet?
_____

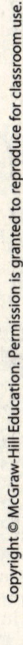

STOP

Weekly Assessment • Unit 5, Week 5   Grade 3   59

UNIT 6 WEEK 1 Name: _____ Date: _____

Read "Prometheus Steals Fire" before you answer Numbers 1 through 5.

Prometheus Steals Fire

> **CHARACTERS**
>
> **Prometheus:** (pro-mee-thee-us) friend of Zeus
> **Zeus:** ruler of the gods
> **Elana:** a peasant woman

SCENE ONE

Zeus's home in Mount Olympus.

PROMETHEUS: Zeus, humans should **possess** fire. They should have it so that they may use it like we do.

ZEUS: No! Humans would become too strong with fire.

SCENE TWO

Outside Elana's home in winter. Prometheus watches.

ELANA: Someone help me! I am in such pain and **anguish** in this cold weather. I cannot bear it any longer.

SCENE THREE

Prometheus steals fire from Zeus and brings it to Elana.

ELANA: Thank you, Prometheus! Now humans can stay warm in winter. We can cook food for our children.

PROMETHEUS: Because of my actions, I can never return to Mount Olympus. But it was the right thing to do.

GO ON →

60 Grade 3   Weekly Assessment • Unit 6, Week 1

Name: _____ Date: _____

Use "Prometheus Steals Fire" to answer Numbers 1 through 5.

1 What does Prometheus want humans to *possess*?
_____
_____

Circle the clues that tell what *possess* means.

2 **Draw a box** around what Zeus says.

Why doesn't Zeus want humans to have fire?
_____
_____

3 **Circle** the word that means almost the SAME as *anguish*.

4 **Underline** the details in the stage directions that tell what Prometheus does for Elana.

5 What is the theme of the play?
_____
_____

Underline a sentence that tells about the theme.

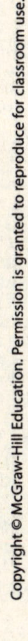

Weekly Assessment • Unit 6, Week 1   Grade 3

UNIT 6 WEEK 2 Name: _____ Date: _____

Read "The Heat Wave of 1896" before you answer Numbers 1 through 5.

The Heat Wave of 1896

In 1896, ice was expensive in New York City. Abby's family did not have much money. One summer day, Abby heard the police were giving away ice to help people survive the hot weather.

Abby's son, Henry, had a fever and needed fresh water badly. But Abby did not want to leave him **stranded** at home. She waited for her daughter to come home. Then she set out to get the ice herself.

Abby headed through the crowded city streets toward the police carriage. She saw hundreds of people waiting in the boiling sun. Hours passed before she received her block of ice. Abby quickly wrapped it in cloth and headed home.

On her way, Abby saw people holding ice to their skin to cool off. She saw the look of **relief** on their faces and imagined how good it would feel to do the same.

But then she remembered Henry. She had been away for hours. What if his fever had gotten worse? Abby walked faster. Henry needed the ice more than she did.

GO ON →

Name: _____ Date: _____

Use "The Heat Wave of 1896" to answer Numbers 1 through 5.

1 Why does Abby need to get ice?

_____

_____

Underline the text evidence.

2 **Circle** the words that help you figure out the meaning of *stranded*.

What does *stranded* mean?

_____

3 **Circle** the sentence that tells how people in the crowd get *relief* from the heat.

What does *relief* mean?

_____

4 **Draw a box** around the details that tell why Abby decides not to stop and rest.

5 What is the theme of this story?

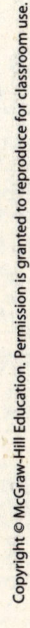

_____

_____

STOP

Weekly Assessment · Unit 6, Week 2   Grade 3   63

UNIT 6 WEEK 3   Name: _____   Date: _____

Read "Astronaut and Role Model" before you answer Numbers 1 through 5.

Astronaut and Role Model

As a child, Mae C. Jemison planned to travel to outer space. One day, she would reach this **goal**. Mae would be the first African American woman to go into space.

In high school, Mae was an excellent student. But some people told her not to study math and science in college. She worked hard to prove them wrong. She went to college and studied math, science, and other subjects. Then, she went on to become a doctor.

After her studies, Mae joined a group to help people around the world. She traveled to where people needed better health care. **Health care** is the care that doctors give people to help them get and stay healthy. Mae became a leader and role model for other medical workers. She also did **research** and tried to find ways to keep people healthy.

Later, Mae joined NASA. She went through difficult training to become an astronaut. In 1992, she went on a mission to space. She did important science experiments during the spaceflight.

Mae tells kids to study math and science. She continues to help others and do great things today.

GO ON →

Name: _____ Date: _____

Use "Astronaut and Role Model" to answer Numbers 1 through 5.

1 **Circle** the *goal* Mae had as a child.

What is a *goal*?
_____

2 **Underline** the problem that Mae had in school.

3 How did Mae solve her problem in college?
_____
_____

4 **Draw a box** around the definition of *health care*.

What steps did Mae take to help solve the *health care* problem?
_____
_____

5 **Circle** the words that help you understand what *research* means.

What does *research* mean?
_____

STOP

Weekly Assessment • Unit 6, Week 3 — Grade 3 — 65

UNIT 6 WEEK 4 Name: _____ Date: _____

Read "Unicorns of the Sea" before you answer Numbers 1 through 5.

Unicorns of the Sea

Whales **inhabit**, or live, in the ocean. All whales are mammals, but only one whale has a long tusk. This whale is the *narwhal*. It is called "the unicorn of the sea."

The narwhal's tusk is **fascinating**. Scientists want to learn more about it. The narwhal has teeth, but unlike other toothed whales, its teeth are not inside its mouth. The male grows a tooth straight from its jaw. This is its tusk. Female narwhals usually do not grow a tusk.

Scientists think the narwhal uses its tusk to compete for females. The tusk's purpose is similar to the purpose of a male deer's antlers or a male peacock's feathers.

All whales are mammals that live in water. They all breathe air. But only the unicorn of the sea has a tusk!

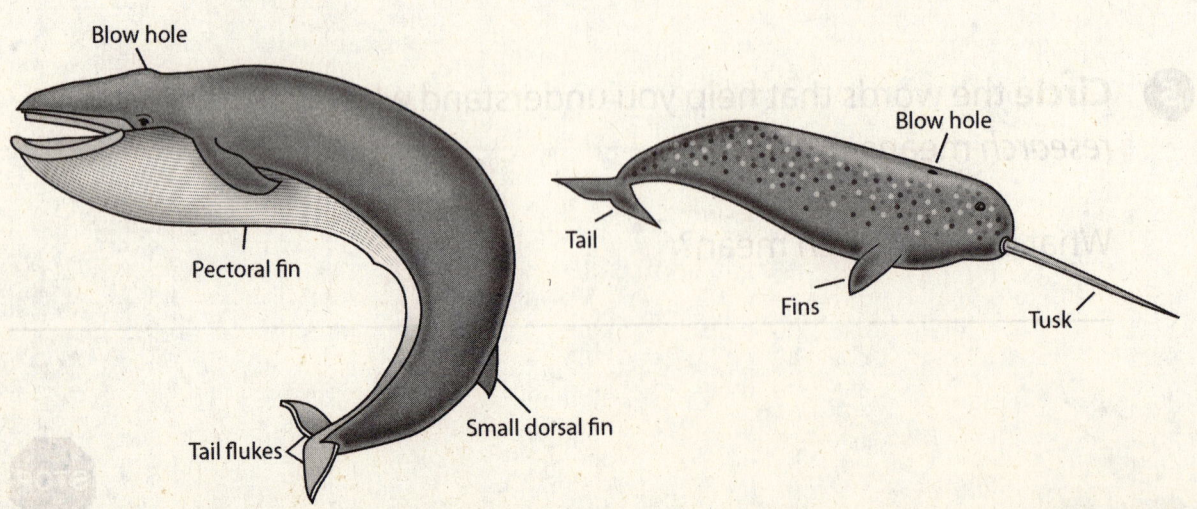

Blue Whale — Blow hole, Pectoral fin, Tail flukes, Small dorsal fin

Narwhal — Blow hole, Tail, Fins, Tusk

GO ON →

66 Grade 3 Weekly Assessment • Unit 6, Week 4

Name: _____ Date: _____

Use "Unicorns of the Sea" to answer Numbers 1 through 5.

1 **Circle** the word that means almost the SAME as *inhabit*.

2 **Underline** how all whales are ALIKE.

How is the narwhal DIFFERENT from other whales?

_____

_____

3 **Circle** the sentence that helps you figure out what *fascinating* means.

What is the meaning of *fascinating*?

_____

4 How is the narwhal's tusk like a male deer's antlers or a male peacock's feathers?

_____

_____

5 Look at the diagrams. List the parts of a narwhal that are SIMILAR to the parts of a blue whale.

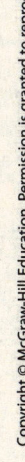

_____

_____

Weekly Assessment • Unit 6, Week 4   Grade 3

UNIT 6 WEEK 5 Name: _____ Date: _____

Read "The Tree's Song" before you answer Numbers 1 through 5.

The Tree's Song

One day I sat beside a tree,
And it began to sing to me.
The song was sweet and made me smile.
I said, "Why, I'll just sit awhile."
I listened to the tree that day,
And watched the branches start to sway
'Til I remembered why I came,
And searched my bag for a new game.

My entertainment was a book.
I took it out and had a look.
Plip plop! Bip Bop! I heard a sound.
I found a lump all big and round.
This was not humorous or fun.
It seemed my time of rest was done!
The tree was dropping nuts on me.
I ran as fast as fast can be!

GO ON →

Name: _____ Date: _____

Use "The Tree's Song" to answer Numbers 1 through 5.

1 What does the narrator think about the tree at the BEGINNING of the poem?
_____

Underline the details.

2 **Draw a box** around the word in the first stanza that has the SAME ending sound as *day*.

What is this called?
_____

3 **Circle** the words that sound like a drumbeat in the second line of the second stanza.

What is this pattern called?
_____

4 What is the narrator's point of view at the END of the poem?
_____

5 How does the story end in this narrative poem?
_____
_____

Weekly Assessment • Unit 6, Week 5

Mid-Unit Assessment

UNIT 1 MID-UNIT

Read "Beaver Building Day" before you answer Numbers 1 through 5.

Beaver Building Day

It was building day in beaver town. Every beaver was supposed to pitch in. Beavers build their homes from sticks and logs. Barry's parents had left early in the morning. They were chewing through big logs. His friends were running around gathering sticks and mud.

But Barry didn't feel like building today. He was sitting in a nice patch of grass in the sun. He wanted to **concentrate** on his book. He was thinking about the story. It was about a bird family. They were looking for a winter home.

Barry heard a voice calling his name. It was his friend Selina. "Barry," she said. "We could use some help over here!"

"I'm not feeling well!" he shouted.

Barry felt bad about lying. But he really wanted to finish his book. In the story, the bird family had found a new place to live. They would stay in Florida. It was nice and warm. They would be safe for the winter. But how would they make a new home?

Barry read breathlessly. The birds had to escape snakes and alligators. Finally, the family worked together to build a new home. They made a nest in a high tree.

GO ON →

Barry finished the book. He had realized something important. There was no time to waste. He ran back home as fast as he could. "Hey, everybody," he called. "I'm here! Do you still need my help?"

"Barry!" Selina called. "Come with me and let's find some more sticks for the roof."

Barry happily helped for the rest of the day. He knew how important it was to have a safe home.

Name: _____ Date: _____

Use "Beaver Building Day" to answer Numbers 1 through 5.

1 Why doesn't Barry want to help during building day?

Ⓐ He does not think homes are important.

Ⓑ He wants to finish reading his book.

Ⓒ He is angry with his parents.

2 Which clue word from the story helps to explain what *concentrate* means?

Ⓐ building

Ⓑ sitting

Ⓒ thinking

3 Which event happens FIRST in the story?

Ⓐ Selina calls to Barry.

Ⓑ Barry says he is sick.

Ⓒ Barry sits in the grass.

GO ON →

Name: _____ Date: _____

4 Which event happens LAST in Barry's book?

Ⓐ The birds build a nest.

Ⓑ The birds escape snakes.

Ⓒ The birds looks for a home.

5 What is the MOST important thing that Barry learns from reading the book?

Ⓐ Some animals are dangerous.

Ⓑ It is important to have a safe home.

Ⓒ Birds move to warm places in winter.

GO ON ➔

Mid-Unit Assessment • Unit 1   Grade 3   75

Read "Making Wontons with Grandpa" before you answer Numbers 6 through 10.

Making Wontons with Grandpa

My favorite memory with my grandfather is making wontons. A wonton is a type of dumpling. It is a wrapped piece of dough with filling inside. Grandpa had learned to make wontons from his parents. Making them would **remind** him of when he was a boy. He had many good memories of his childhood.

Grandpa owned a restaurant. I would watch him fold the wontons so quickly that his fingers were a blur. One day he showed me how.

We stood in the kitchen. On the counter sat a bowl with filling for the wontons. It smelled delicious. It had meat and onions. The square wonton wrappers were under a towel. Grandpa said that it kept them moist. They wouldn't dry out. There was also a bowl with eggs that were beaten.

Grandpa took one square wrapper in his hand. Then he took a teaspoon of filling. He placed it in the center. He dipped a brush in the eggs. Then he wet the edges of the wrapper. This would make them stick together. He brushed on a little more egg. Then he pressed the edges of the wonton together. It now looked a little like a fortune cookie. The wonton was ready.

GO ON →

It was my turn. I was nervous. I folded my first wonton. It looked uneven. Grandpa helped me fix the edges. After **practicing**, my wontons looked better. I needed to try many times to learn.

At last, all the wontons were ready. Grandpa placed them in a hot broth. They cooked for a few minutes. He put the hot soup and wontons into bowls.

I tried a sip. "Mmm," I said. It was the only sound I could make.

Grandpa smiled. "One day, you can teach your children," he said.

I know that I will.

Name: _____ Date: _____

Use "Making Wontons with Grandpa" to answer Numbers 6 through 10.

6 Read these sentences from the passage.

> Grandpa had learned to make wontons from his parents. Making them would remind him of when he was a boy. He had many good memories of his childhood.

Which phrase from the sentences helps to explain the meaning of *remind*?

Ⓐ had learned

Ⓑ making them

Ⓒ good memories

7 What is the FIRST step in making wontons?

Ⓐ Place the filling in the center of the wonton.

Ⓑ Hold the wonton wrapper in one hand.

Ⓒ Wet the edges of the wonton wrapper.

8 What should be done RIGHT AFTER brushing the edges of the wrapper with egg?

Ⓐ Press the edges of the wonton together.

Ⓑ Dip the brush into the beaten eggs.

Ⓒ Cook the wontons in a broth.

GO ON ➔

78   Grade 3   Mid-Unit Assessment • Unit 1

Name: _____   Date: _____

9 Read these sentences from the passage.

> **After practicing, my wontons looked better.
> I needed to try many times to learn.**

Which phrase from the sentences gives a clue about the meaning of *practicing*?

Ⓐ looked better

Ⓑ I needed

Ⓒ try many times

10 What is the LAST thing the author does?

Ⓐ He makes wontons.

Ⓑ He eats wonton soup.

Ⓒ He tells what a wonton is.

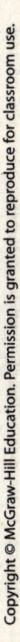

STOP

Mid-Unit Assessment • Unit 1   Grade 3   79

UNIT 2 MID-UNIT

Read "A Long Way from Home" before you answer Numbers 1 through 5.

A Long Way from Home

"Ramon, don't cut yourself," said Ron. He looked at the sharp tool in Ramon's hand.

"We need to clean six fish a minute. I must work fast," said Ramon.

"But you look tired," replied Ron.

"I am fine. This is our job. We clean fish. I do not want to lose this job," said Ramon.

The year was 1922. Ron and Ramon worked in a fish cannery in Alaska. A cannery is a place where people clean and cut fish. Then they put the fish in cans. There were no machines to do it. It was hard work. The place smelled bad. The work days were long.

After work, Ramon looked at **photographs**. They were pictures of his family. They lived far away in the Philippines. He missed them. Ramon and Ron's trip on the ship to Alaska was long.

"Ramon, do you miss home?" asked Ron.

"Yes. I miss my family. But someday I will go to college. Then I will get a good job. I will have my family come here," said Ramon.

GO ON →

"I remember we came here to go to college. Now all we do is work," said Ron.

"We make so little money. It is hard to save. It will take time to pay for college," replied Ramon.

Ramon tried to guess how long he would have to work at this hard job. "I **estimate** it will take a year to save the money for college," he said. But hard work would never make him give up.

Name: _____ Date: _____

Use "A Long Way from Home" to answer Numbers 1 through 5.

1 What is the theme of this story?

   Ⓐ Working in a cannery in Alaska is a good job.

   Ⓑ People miss home when they have to go away.

   Ⓒ Sometimes we must work to make our dreams come true.

2 Which sentence BEST supports the idea that Ramon and Ron have a difficult job?

   Ⓐ They must clean six fish a minute.

   Ⓑ They took a ship to get to Alaska.

   Ⓒ They think about their families.

3 Read these sentences from the story.

   After work, Ramon looked at photographs. They were pictures of his family.

   Which word from the sentences helps you understand the meaning of *photographs*?

   Ⓐ looked

   Ⓑ pictures

   Ⓒ family

GO ON →

82 Grade 3   Mid-Unit Assessment • Unit 2

Name: _____ Date: _____

4 Which sentence from the text BEST supports the story's theme?

Ⓐ Ron and Ramon worked in a fish cannery in Alaska.

Ⓑ They lived far away in the Philippines.

Ⓒ But hard work would never make him give up.

5 Read these sentences from the story.

> **Ramon tried to guess how long he would have to work at this hard job. "I estimate it will take a year to save the money for college," he said.**

Which phrase from the sentences helps you understand the meaning of *estimate*?

Ⓐ tried to guess

Ⓑ work at this hard job

Ⓒ save the money

Mid-Unit Assessment • Unit 2

GO ON ➔

Grade 3 83

Read "Our Government" before you answer Numbers 6 through 10.

Our Government

The U.S. President is elected every four years. He runs the whole country. The country has a big government. It helps the President. Every state and city has a government, too. These governments help the bigger government and the President.

The President runs all 50 states. Each state has a governor. The people of a state elect their governor. The governor manages that state. Governors can pass laws for that state only. Governors cannot pass laws for the whole country.

A mayor is a person who runs a town or city. Mayors are elected by the people of the city. They report to the governor of their state.

There is also a city council. It helps the mayor. Several people are elected to the council. The council helps pass new laws for the city. They think of new ways to help the city. They listen to the people. The mayor and the council get **involved** with the people. They take part in fixing people's problems.

Mayors lead many city departments. These departments help people. Mayors are in charge of the police. They also run the fire department.

GO ON →

The mayor controls transportation, as well. This includes buses and subways. The mayor also controls public works. Public works help to keep the city clean. They pick up garbage. They also fix streets. The mayor even runs city parks.

The mayor picks leaders for these departments. These people report to the mayor. Mayors are important parts of government.

State and Local Jobs

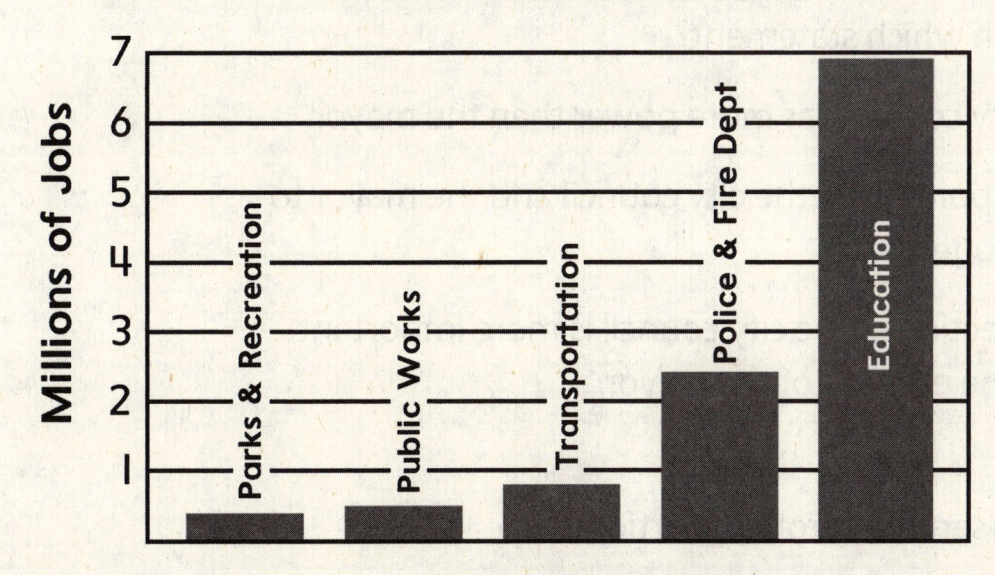

Millions of Jobs / Types of Jobs

- Parks & Recreation
- Public Works
- Transportation
- Police & Fire Dept
- Education

Name: _____ Date: _____

Use "Our Government" to answer Numbers 6 through 10.

6 Which sentence from the article shows what the author thinks about mayors?

Ⓐ They report to the governor of their state.

Ⓑ Mayors are in charge of the police.

Ⓒ Mayors are important parts of government.

7 Based on the article, the author would MOST LIKELY agree with which statement?

Ⓐ The city council has more power than the mayor.

Ⓑ It is important for the city council and the mayor to work together.

Ⓒ The election of the city council is more important than the election of the mayor.

8 Read this sentence from the article.

The mayor and the council get involved with the people.

Which phrase from the article helps you understand the meaning of *involved*?

Ⓐ helps pass new laws

Ⓑ think of new ways

Ⓒ take part in fixing

GO ON →

86 Grade 3 Mid-Unit Assessment • Unit 2

Name: _____ Date: _____

9 With which statement would the author MOST LIKELY agree?

Ⓐ A mayor helps to keep a city safe.

Ⓑ A mayor is as important as the President.

Ⓒ A mayor does not work as hard as a governor.

10 According to the bar graph, which type of job has the MOST workers?

Ⓐ Education

Ⓑ Public Works

Ⓒ Transportation

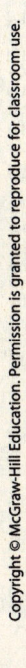

Read "Sea Turtle and Hermit Crab" before you answer Numbers 1 through 5.

Sea Turtle and Hermit Crab

A long time ago, there was a young sea turtle. He lived deep in the ocean. At this time, sea turtles didn't have shells. Sea Turtle was scared of many things. He was very delicate. His neighbor was Hermit Crab. Hermit Crab had a beautiful shell. He loved to boast about it. Sea Turtle and Hermit Crab were quite opposite. But they had one thing in common. They were both scared of King Shark.

One day, Hermit Crab was admiring his shell. Then along came King Shark. Hermit Crab didn't notice. He was too busy looking at himself.

King Shark swam at Hermit Crab. He chomped his jaws with a loud snap.

"Aaah!" screamed Hermit Crab. "Help me!"

Sea Turtle heard the cry. He quickly went to help Hermit Crab.

King Shark had Hermit Crab in his jaws. Hermit Crab thought his shell would break! But Sea Turtle kicked King Shark in the nose. Stunned, King Shark let go. He swam in circles. He made a big wave of bubbles.

"Come, quick!" Sea Turtle said. "We must hide."

Sea Turtle and Hermit Crab hid under a rock. King Shark searched furiously. But the danger was **temporary**. King Shark swam away after only a short time. Then, Sea Turtle and Hermit Crab returned home.

"You save me!" Hermit Crab said. "But my shell has gone flat from King Shark's bite. It does not fit me any more. Here, you take it."

From that day on, Sea Turtle always had a beautiful shell. He was happy, but he never boasted.

That is how the sea turtle got its shell. And that is why the hermit crab always looks for new shells. He hopes to find a prettier one than the one he lost.

Name: _____ Date: _____

Use "Sea Turtle and Hermit Crab" to answer Numbers 1 through 5.

1 What is Sea Turtle's problem at the beginning of the story?

  Ⓐ He lives in the ocean.

  Ⓑ He has no shell.

  Ⓒ He boasts a lot.

2 What happens to Hermit Crab when the shark bites him?

  Ⓐ His shell falls off.

  Ⓑ His shell becomes flatter.

  Ⓒ His shell becomes bigger.

3 What causes Hermit Crab to look for a new shell?

  Ⓐ He wants to find one as beautiful as his old one.

  Ⓑ He wants to give the new shell to Sea Turtle.

  Ⓒ He does not want King Shark to bite him.

GO ON →

90 Grade 3   Mid-Unit Assessment • Unit 3

Name: _____ Date: _____

4 Read these sentences from the story.

> **But the danger was temporary. King Shark swam away after only a short time.**

Which clue words in the sentences help to explain the meaning of *temporary*?

Ⓐ the danger

Ⓑ swam away

Ⓒ only a short time

5 How is Sea Turtle's problem solved?

Ⓐ Sea Turtle receives Hermit Crab's shell.

Ⓑ King Shark gives Sea Turtle a shell.

Ⓒ Sea Turtle makes a new shell.

Mid-Unit Assessment • Unit 3

GO ON ➔

Grade 3   91

Read "Jupiter" before you answer Numbers 6 through 10.

Jupiter

There are eight planets in our solar system. Jupiter is the fifth planet from the Sun. It is the largest planet. It is more than 1,000 times bigger than Earth!

It is very stormy on Jupiter. There are storms all the time. There are many clouds. This makes Jupiter very colorful. There are bands of red and orange.

Jupiter has a giant red spot. It is called the "Eye of Jupiter." It is a giant storm. It has been going on for 300 years. The storm covers an area larger than Earth!

Jupiter is a gas giant. It does not have a solid **surface**, or outer layer. It is made up of hydrogen and water. There is no place to stand on Jupiter!

You might think that Saturn is the only planet with rings. But Jupiter has rings, too. They are hard to see. You can see them when Jupiter passes in front of the Sun. There are three rings in all. They are named Gossamer, Main, and Halo.

Jupiter also has a lot of moons. There are 50 in all! The four largest moons are called Io, Europa, Ganymede, and Callisto. They were discovered by a famous scientist named Galileo. He discovered them in 1610.

GO ON →

Sometimes, you can see Jupiter just by looking up at the sky. With a telescope, you can see its moons. The next time you look through a telescope, try to find this **splendid**, wonderful planet!

Planet (listed by distance from Sun)	Diameter (kilometers)
Venus	12,104 km
Earth	12,756 km
Mars	6,788 km
Mercury	4,880 km
Jupiter	142,740 km
Saturn	120,034 km
Uranus	51,152 km
Neptune	49,620 km

Name: _____ Date: _____

Use "Jupiter" to answer Numbers 6 through 10.

6 Read this sentence from the article.

> **Jupiter is a gas giant.**

Which detail from the article supports this sentence?

Ⓐ Jupiter is the fifth planet from the Sun.

Ⓑ There is no place to stand on Jupiter!

Ⓒ But Jupiter has rings, too.

7 Which words in the article mean almost the SAME as *surface*?

Ⓐ red spot

Ⓑ giant storm

Ⓒ outer layer

8 Which sentence describes the MAIN idea of the article?

Ⓐ There are eight planets in our solar system.

Ⓑ Jupiter is an amazing planet.

Ⓒ Jupiter has 50 moons.

GO ON →

Name: _____ Date: _____

9 Read this sentence from the article.

> **The next time you look through a telescope, try to find this splendid, wonderful planet!**

Which clue word in the sentence helps to explain the meaning of *splendid*?

Ⓐ look

Ⓑ telescope

Ⓒ wonderful

10 According to the chart, which is the smallest planet in our solar system?

Ⓐ Mercury

Ⓑ Uranus

Ⓒ Venus

Mid-Unit Assessment • Unit 3   Grade 3   95

UNIT 4 MID-UNIT

Read "Rainforest Berries" before you answer Numbers 1 through 5.

Rainforest Berries

I was pretty excited. I was visiting the rainforest for the first time! I read all about it before I left my family's house in Seattle. I wanted to recognize any plants or animals I saw. My cousins were riding in the car with me. They visited their family's cabin in the Cascade Mountains every year. I wanted to ask them what lived and grew in the woods. But they were sleeping or listening to music.

Finally, we got to the cabin. The forest looked awesome! Weird moss hung like fur from the pine trees. I couldn't wait to explore!

After we unpacked the car, my cousins went inside. For about an hour, they sat and played video games. I sat with them for a while. But soon I was bored.

"Want to go outside?" I asked.

"And do what?" my cousin Todd asked. "We come here every year. We've seen all there is to see."

I pretended to believe him. "Maybe you could show me around the woods, then," I suggested.

We all went outside. I looked around to see if I recognized any plants. I spotted a bush with pink flowers on it. It looked exactly like a plant I had seen in a book.

GO ON →

"Is this a salmonberry bush?" I asked.

My cousins shrugged.

I reached into it and picked some orange and red berries. "The red ones aren't as **flavorful** as the orange ones. But the orange ones are supposed to be tasty," I said.

Todd looked surprised. "I didn't know you could eat stuff in this forest," he said.

"There's always more to learn about stuff," I said. "Even if something's familiar, that doesn't mean you've learned everything there is to know about it."

I was a little proud of myself. I had identified one of the plants I had read about! I set out to find more with new **confidence**.

Name: _____ Date: _____

Use "Rainforest Berries" to answer Numbers 1 through 5.

1 Why aren't the narrator's cousins interested in exploring the forest?

Ⓐ They think they have seen everything in the forest.

Ⓑ They have already read books about the forest.

Ⓒ They are tired after the car ride.

2 How does the narrator change Todd's point of view about the rainforest?

Ⓐ by showing how the rainforest is more interesting than video games

Ⓑ by showing there are things left to learn about the rainforest

Ⓒ by showing how to identify plants in the rainforest

3 Read these sentences from the story.

> "The red ones aren't as flavorful as the orange ones. But the orange ones are supposed to be tasty," I said.

Which word from the sentences helps you understand the meaning of *flavorful*?

Ⓐ red

Ⓑ supposed

Ⓒ tasty

GO ON →

98   Grade 3   Mid-Unit Assessment • Unit 4

4 Read this paragraph from the story.

> I was a little proud of myself. I had identified one of the plants I had read about. I set out to find more with new confidence.

Which phrase from the paragraph helps you understand the meaning of *confidence*?

Ⓐ proud of myself

Ⓑ identified one of the plants

Ⓒ set out to find more

5 What is the narrator's point of view about learning at the end of the story?

Ⓐ You need to travel in order to learn.

Ⓑ You won't learn anything if you don't go outside.

Ⓒ You can always learn more, even about things that are familiar.

GO ON →

Mid-Unit Assessment · Unit 4

UNIT 4 MID-UNIT

Read "Owls and Their Habitats" before you answer Numbers 6 through 10.

Owls and Their Habitats

All owls share many qualities. But owls live all around the world. They survive in many environments. Each species has adapted in their own ways. For that reason, many owls look different from others.

The Snowy Owl lives in the cold North. It nests in the Arctic tundra. The tundra is cold and flat. Snowy Owls cannot always find food there. So they fly south. There, they hunt in the forests. They eat mice, rabbits, and other animals.

The Snowy Owl has adapted to its cold home. It has thick feathers. This thick coat keeps it warm. Its color helps it survive, too. Snowy Owls are mostly white. This helps them blend in with the snow. Animals do not see them. Female snowy owls have many brown spots. These help when they lay eggs. The tundra is not as snowy as the forest. The spots help them blend with the grass and shrubs. Predators are less likely to see them.

The White-fronted Scops Owl has a very different home. It lives in southeast Asia. It hunts in the rainforests there. These forests are very different from the tundra. They are very hot. They get lots of rain. Many trees grow there.

GO ON →

The White-fronted Scops Owl is very good at hiding in the rainforest. It is a small, brown owl. It has big, yellow eyes. It spends the day in trees. When it closes its eyes, its feathers match the tree bark. Animals cannot see it well. It can also press its feathers to its body. This makes the owl much thinner. It looks very much like a branch! This works very well. It give the owl **excellent** camouflage.

The Scops Owl and the Snowy Owl are both owls. But their habitats are very different. Each one has adapted in its own way.

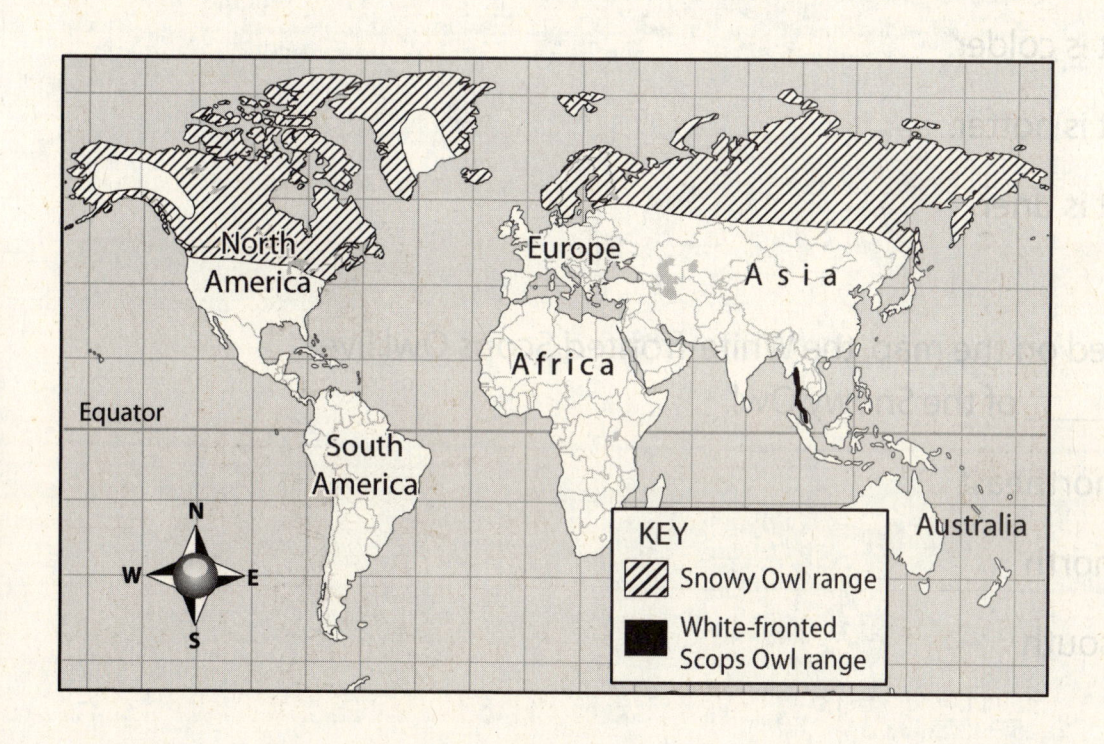

Name: _____ Date: _____

Use "Owls and Their Habitats" to answer Numbers 6 through 10.

6 This article compares two owl species by showing how each species _____.

Ⓐ hides from its prey

Ⓑ lives looks the same

Ⓒ has adapted to survive

7 How is a White-fronted Scops Owl's habitat DIFFERENT from a Snowy Owl's habitat?

Ⓐ It is colder.

Ⓑ It is hotter.

Ⓒ It is drier.

8 Based on the map, the White-fronted Scops Owl lives _____ of the Snowy Owl.

Ⓐ northeast

Ⓑ north

Ⓒ south

GO ON →

102 Grade 3   Mid-Unit Assessment • Unit 4

Name: _____ Date: _____

9 Read these sentences from the article.

> It looks very much like a branch! This works very well. It gives the owl excellent camouflage.

Which phrase from the sentences helps you understand the meaning of *excellent*?

Ⓐ like a branch

Ⓑ works very well

Ⓒ gives the owl

10 How are White-fronted Scops Owls and Snowy Owls ALIKE?

Ⓐ They both have colors that help them blend with their surroundings.

Ⓑ They both can change the shape of their bodies to help them hide.

Ⓒ They both fly south to hunt for food.

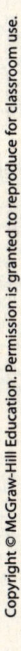

UNIT 5 MID-UNIT

Read "The Silver Moneybag" before you answer Numbers 1 through 5.

The Silver Moneybag

Long ago, Kip and Hana were a husband and wife who lived in a small hut. They were very poor. Every day, they cut two bundles of firewood. They sold one at the market. The other, they kept in the kitchen for themselves.

One morning, a bundle was missing. Kip and Hana had to sell their only firewood. The next day, it happened again. The couple was cold, so Kip came up with a plan.

That night, he made a hollow in the bundle of firewood and hid inside it. At midnight, he saw a little old man approach and start to drag away the bundle. Kip leaped out, startling him.

"Please, sir," Kip said. "We need this firewood." He explained that they were very poor.

The old man was sheepish. He said, "I'm sorry. Here, take this bag. But remember, you must take only one piece of silver each day." And then he was gone.

Once Kip got home, he gave the bag to Hana. She reached inside and pulled out one silver piece! Each night they would take one piece of silver. These they saved carefully.

GO ON →

One day, Kip said, "Let's build ourselves a bigger cottage."

Hana responded, "No, Kip. We don't yet have enough silver for that."

Kip paused. Finally, he nodded **reluctantly**. That night after Hana had gone to sleep, Kip reached into the bag an extra time. An extra silver piece rolled out. He opened it again and again. Soon he had a mountain of silver, enough to build a fine house!

That morning, he rushed to get Hana to show her the pile. Instead, there was no silver **remaining**. It was all gone.

Hana tried to make Kip feel better. "We cannot depend on a silver moneybag," she said. "Let's go back to the mountain and chop firewood as we did before. That is a dependable way to earn a living."

Name: _____ Date: _____

Use "The Silver Moneybag" to answer Numbers 1 through 5.

1 What is Kip's point of view about the moneybag?

Ⓐ He wants to keep saving the coins.

Ⓑ He wants to give the coins to the old man.

Ⓒ He wants to use the coins to build a new house.

2 What is Hana's point of view about the moneybag?

Ⓐ She wants to continue to take only what is needed.

Ⓑ She wants to use all of the coins to buy more firewood.

Ⓒ She wants to return the moneybag to its rightful owner.

3 Read these sentences from the story.

Kip paused. Finally, he nodded reluctantly.

Which clue word from the sentences helps to explain the meaning of *reluctantly*?

Ⓐ paused

Ⓑ he

Ⓒ nodded

GO ON ➔

106   Grade 3   Mid-Unit Assessment • Unit 5

Name: _____ Date: _____

4 Read these sentences from the story.

> **Instead, there was no silver remaining.
> It was all gone.**

Which word from the sentences means about the OPPOSITE of *remaining*?

Ⓐ instead

Ⓑ silver

Ⓒ gone

5 Which sentence shows Hana's point of view at the end of the story?

Ⓐ Money is not that important.

Ⓑ Money is not real if it is not earned.

Ⓒ Money should be earned through work.

GO ON →

Mid-Unit Assessment • Unit 5 Grade 3 107

Read "A Restaurant Team" before you answer Numbers 6 through 10.

A Restaurant Team

You go to a busy restaurant. You are welcomed at the door. Then your order is taken. Someone takes your plate away when you are done. You see many workers.

There are also restaurant workers you do not see. These workers are in the kitchen. They prepare your food for you.

Every restaurant worker has an important job. Each team member has a **purpose**.

Host

The host is the first person you see. The host greets customers and finds them a table. The host also takes phone reservations.

Manager

The manager has the most important job in a restaurant. The manager is in charge and does all the hiring. The manager also helps other team members.

Waitperson

Waiters and waitresses bring you menus. They write down orders. They bring that order to the kitchen. Then they bring your food when it is ready. They check on you during your meal. They want to make sure that everything tastes good.

GO ON →

Busser

Bussers clear your table after your meal. They bring you ketchup or more napkins. They refill your water glass.

Chef

The chef is another important team member. The chef cooks the food. He or she is often the person who creates the menu. The chef also finds and buys the ingredients.

Assistant Chef

An assistant chef helps the chef prepare the meal. This includes chopping vegetables and making soup broth.

Dishwasher

The dishwasher washes the dishes. Dishwashers often become bussers after a few months on the job.

All of these workers help make your meal enjoyable. A great team works together to make a good restaurant run smoothly.

Name: _____   Date: _____

Use "A Restaurant Team" to answer Numbers 6 through 10.

6 Read this paragraph from the article.

> Every restaurant worker has an important job to do. Each team member has a purpose.

Which phrase from the paragraph helps to explain the meaning of *purpose*?

Ⓐ restaurant worker

Ⓑ important job

Ⓒ team member

7 Which sentence from the article BEST shows what the author thinks about restaurant managers?

Ⓐ The manager has the most important job in a restaurant.

Ⓑ The manager is in charge and does all the hiring.

Ⓒ The manager also helps other team members.

GO ON →

Name: _____ Date: _____

8 Read these sentences from the article.

> **The chef is another important team member.**
> **The chef cooks the food.**

What does the author MOST LIKELY think about chefs?

Ⓐ The chef is in charge of everyone in a restaurant.

Ⓑ The chef has the simplest job in a restaurant.

Ⓒ The chef is necessary in a restaurant.

9 Which section of the article tells about the team member who deals with a meal order?

Ⓐ Host

Ⓑ Waitperson

Ⓒ Assistant Chef

10 Which sentence in the text helps you figure out why the author wrote this article?

Ⓐ There are also restaurant workers you do not see.

Ⓑ They want to make sure that everything tastes good.

Ⓒ A great team works together to make a good restaurant run smoothly.

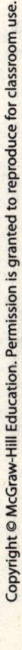

Mid-Unit Assessment • Unit 5   Grade 3   111

UNIT 6 MID-UNIT

Read "The Great Hailstorm" before you answer Numbers 1 through 5.

The Great Hailstorm

It was September 2, 1960. This morning, there was a good reason to jump out of bed. I was **motivated** to get downstairs because it was my tenth birthday!

My mom had been planning a party for me. She had all the **necessary**, or required, food for it. All my friends were going to come. Many of my uncles and aunts from southern California were coming, too.

I think my brother Billy was jealous that it was my birthday. Billy said, "I hope it rains!" Then we had a big fight. He took off on a bicycle to his friend's house. I was so mad that I hoped he would stay there. I didn't want him at my party.

Then, I went to the backyard to start setting up the games for my party. But there were dark clouds moving overhead. "We can play games inside," my mom said, trying to make me feel better. I heard a loud clap of thunder as my mom hurried me inside.

I was standing in the kitchen when I heard a loud sound, like rocks hitting the roof. I rushed to the window to look outside. It was a hailstorm! Balls of ice were falling from the sky. They were the size of golf balls. I looked out the front window. My mother's car was being dented by the hail.

GO ON →

Suddenly, I thought about Billy. Was he okay? My mom was about to call his friend's house when he came in through the garage. Mom and I sighed in relief. He said, "I'm so sorry about your party."

"I can always have another party," I said. "The most important thing is that you're safe!"

Name: _____ Date: _____

Use "The Great Hailstorm" to answer Numbers 1 through 5.

1 Read these sentences from the story.

> This morning, there was a good reason to jump out of bed. I was motivated to get downstairs because it was my tenth birthday!

Which phrase from the sentences helps to explain the meaning of *motivated*?

Ⓐ this morning

Ⓑ good reason to

Ⓒ get downstairs

2 Read these sentences from the story.

> My mom had been planning a party for me. She had all the necessary, or required, food for it.

Which word from the sentences helps you understand the meaning of *necessary*?

Ⓐ planning

Ⓑ required

Ⓒ food

GO ON →

114 Grade 3

Mid-Unit Assessment • Unit 6

Name: _____ Date: _____

3 What do you learn from the story about being part of a family?

Ⓐ It is more important to think of your family than to think only of yourself.

Ⓑ Sometimes family members live in other parts of the country.

Ⓒ People live together in families.

4 Which action by the narrator BEST describes the lesson of this story?

Ⓐ Then, I went to the backyard to start setting up the games for my party.

Ⓑ I rushed to the window to look outside.

Ⓒ Suddenly, I thought about Billy.

5 Which sentence from the text BEST describes the story's lesson?

Ⓐ "I hope it rains!"

Ⓑ "I can always have another party," I said.

Ⓒ "The most important thing is that you're safe!"

GO ON →

Mid-Unit Assessment • Unit 6

Read "Captain Meriwether Lewis" before you answer Numbers 6 through 10.

Captain Meriwether Lewis

Early Life

Meriwether Lewis was born in Virginia on August 18, 1774. As a child, he liked hunting and learning about nature. He also wanted to travel and explore. Later, he joined the army. There he met William Clark. After several years, Lewis was picked to work for the President of the United States. The President was Thomas Jefferson.

The Louisiana Purchase

President Jefferson bought a giant piece of land from France in 1803. This new land was west of the Mississippi River. It was called the Louisiana Purchase.

Jefferson did not know anything about this land. He wanted a group to explore it. He wanted to know about the animals and plants that lived there. He also wanted to know about the people there.

Jefferson wanted to know if there was a way across the land to get to the Pacific Ocean. He chose Lewis to explore this new land. He wanted Lewis to find a way to the Pacific Ocean.

Explorer

Lewis asked Clark to help him lead the expedition. An **expedition** is a journey that explores new places. They left from St. Louis, Missouri, in 1804.

Lewis and Clark had to deal with terrible **conditions** while traveling. They found themselves in bad circumstances. There were dangerous rivers and bad storms. They were often sick and hurt.

Lewis met many Native Americans. They helped his group by giving Lewis supplies. Later, a young Native American joined their group. Her name was Sacagawea. She helped Lewis talk to other Native Americans.

Finally, the group reached the Pacific Ocean. Lewis was a hero when he returned to St. Louis. The group was gone for two years. Lewis had found a route to the Pacific Ocean. He also had brought back many new plants and animals from the trip.

Name: _____ Date: _____

Use "Captain Meriwether Lewis" to answer Numbers 6 through 10.

6 What was President Jefferson's MAIN problem with the Louisiana Purchase?

Ⓐ He did not know anything about the new land.

Ⓑ The land was west of the Mississippi River.

Ⓒ He bought the land from France.

7 What is the definition of the keyword *expedition*?

Ⓐ terrible weather

Ⓑ dangerous rivers and bad storms

Ⓒ a journey that explores new places

8 Read these sentences from the article.

> Lewis and Clark had to deal with terrible conditions while traveling. They found themselves in bad circumstances.

Which word from the sentences means about the SAME as *conditions*?

Ⓐ traveling

Ⓑ bad

Ⓒ circumstances

GO ON →

118 Grade 3   Mid-Unit Assessment • Unit 6

Name: _____ Date: _____

9 How did Sacagawea solve the problem of Lewis not being able to talk with other Native Americans?

Ⓐ She traveled with him.

Ⓑ She gave him helpful supplies.

Ⓒ She told him about the Pacific Ocean.

10 What problem did Lewis solve for President Jefferson?

Ⓐ He met many Native Americans.

Ⓑ He returned a hero after two years.

Ⓒ He found a route to the Pacific Ocean.

Name: _____ Date: _____

9. How did Sacagawea solve the problem of Lewis not being able to talk with other Native Americans?

Ⓐ She traveled with him.

Ⓑ She gave him helpful supplies.

Ⓒ She told him about the Pacific Ocean.

10. What problem did Lewis solve for President Jefferson?

Ⓐ He met many Native Americans.

Ⓑ He returned a hero after two years.

Ⓒ He found a route to the Pacific Ocean.

Unit Assessment

UNIT 1

Read "A Pig for Good Luck" before you answer Numbers 1 through 7.

A Pig for Good Luck

Liz walked home from school. Her head was down. She was on the track team, and her first race was coming up. She did not know if she could win the race. Liz did not feel brave. She needed to find some **courage**.

"Uncle Rob came today," Liz thought. "He will cheer me up!"

Uncle Rob lived in Chile. That is a country in South America. Rob visited Liz's family every year. He always made Liz laugh.

When Liz got home, she gave her uncle a big hug.

"I have a gift for you," Uncle Rob said. He reached into his bag. Then he held out a small toy. It was a little clay pig.

Liz looked at the pig in surprise. "It only has three legs!" she said.

Her uncle smiled. "This little pig is from a village in Chile. The people who made it say that it will bring good luck. It is a custom to give it to friends and family."

Liz took the pig. That night she put it on her desk. She hoped her uncle was right.

GO ON →

Name: _____ Date: _____

Liz was not afraid to race the next day. She did not feel **scared**. She showed up with the little pig in her hand. When the whistle blew, she ran ahead of all the others. After the race, she thanked her uncle.

"The pig really was good luck!" she said.

Use "A Pig for Good Luck" to answer Numbers 1 through 7.

1 How does Liz feel at the BEGINNING of the story?

Ⓐ confused

Ⓑ lonely

Ⓒ worried

2 Read this sentence from the story.

She needed to find some courage.

Which sentence from the story gives a clue about the meaning of *courage*?

Ⓐ Her head was down.

Ⓑ Liz did not feel brave.

Ⓒ He always made Liz laugh.

GO ON →

Unit Assessment • Unit 1 Grade 3 123

3 What happens AFTER Uncle Rob gives Liz a pig?

Ⓐ Liz runs in her first race.

Ⓑ Uncle Rob visits from Chile.

Ⓒ Liz walks home from school.

4 How does Liz feel when she FIRST sees the pig?

Ⓐ excited

Ⓑ surprised

Ⓒ thankful

5 How does Uncle Rob help Liz?

Ⓐ He smiles at her.

Ⓑ He makes her laugh.

Ⓒ He gives her a lucky gift.

GO ON →

Name: _____ Date: _____

6 Read these sentences from the story.

**Liz was not afraid to race the next day.
She did not feel scared.**

Which word from these sentences helps you understand the meaning of *scared*?

Ⓐ afraid

Ⓑ race

Ⓒ next

7 What does Liz do RIGHT AFTER the whistle blows in the story?

Ⓐ She puts the pig in her hand.

Ⓑ She runs ahead of the others.

Ⓒ She thanks her uncle for the gift.

Read "Central Park" before you answer Numbers 8 through 15.

Central Park

Central Park is a big park. This **grand** place is in New York City. It is there so that people can enjoy nature in the city. They sit on green grass under trees. But many people do not know how Central Park came to be.

In 1857, people decided that they wanted a park. So, a group held a contest. People tried to come up with plans for the park. A plan was finally chosen.

But there was a problem. The land was rocky. It was wet and muddy. The soil was a poor **quality**. It could not grow trees.

So, soil was brought in from New Jersey. Workers dug up the land. They got rid of big rocks. Soon, bridges and lakes were made. Trees were planted. The park was ready!

But by the 1920s, the park was in bad shape. As a result, a man named Robert Moses was hired. He fixed the park.

Soon, it was full of life again. Flowers bloomed. Fountains worked. Playgrounds, ball fields, and statues were built. People even started acting in plays in the park. It became a fun place again.

GO ON →

Central Park was named a national **landmark** in 1962. The government realized that the park is an important place. Today, people from around the world come to see it.

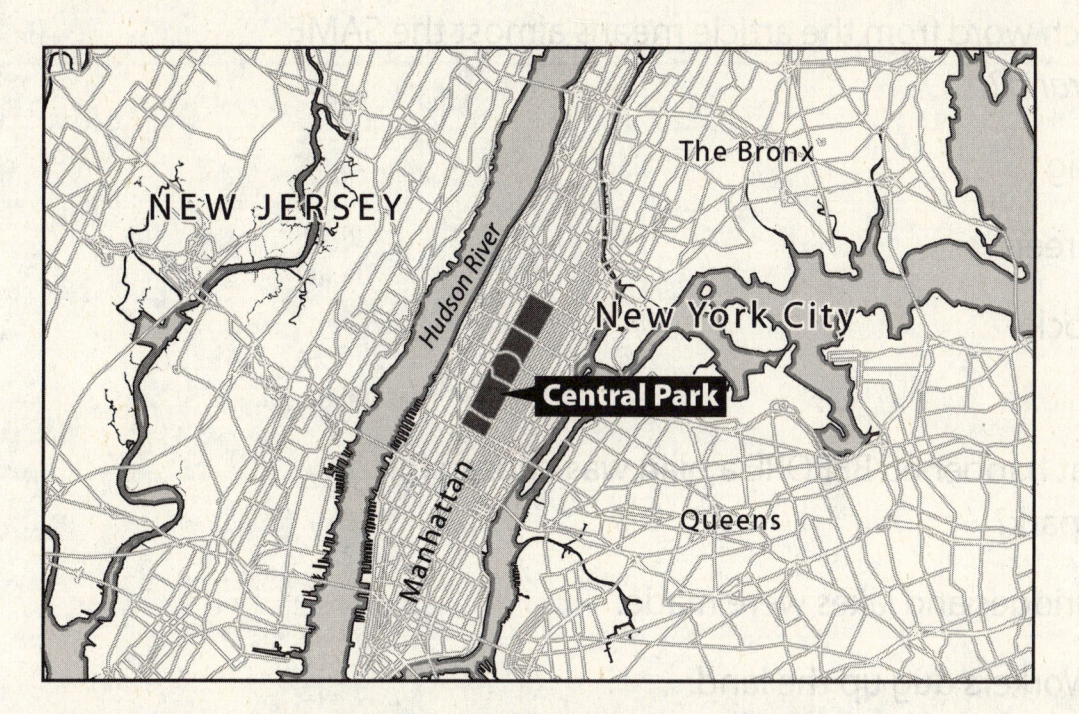

Central Park takes up 51 city blocks.

Name: _____ Date: _____

Use "Central Park" to answer Numbers 8 through 15.

8 Read this sentence from the article.

This grand place is in New York City.

Which word from the article means almost the SAME as *grand*?

Ⓐ big

Ⓑ green

Ⓒ rocky

9 What happened BEFORE a plan was chosen for the park?

Ⓐ Bridges and lakes were made.

Ⓑ Workers dug up the land.

Ⓒ A group held a contest.

10 When was Robert Moses hired?

Ⓐ in 1857

Ⓑ in the 1920s

Ⓒ in 1962

GO ON →

Name: _____ Date: _____

11 Read this sentence from the article.

The soil was a poor quality.

Which words from the article help you understand the meaning of *quality*?

Ⓐ was finally chosen

Ⓑ could not grow trees

Ⓒ park was ready

12 How did Robert Moses help Central Park?

Ⓐ He made it look better.

Ⓑ He drew many pictures of it.

Ⓒ He told the government about it.

13 Read this sentence from the article.

Central Park was named a national landmark in 1962.

Which words from the article help you understand the meaning of *landmark*?

Ⓐ full of life

Ⓑ important place

Ⓒ around the world

GO ON →

Unit Assessment • Unit 1   Grade 3   129

Name: _____ Date: _____

14 Which sentence describes the MAIN idea of the article?

Ⓐ Central Park is a very big park.

Ⓑ Central Park needed to be improved.

Ⓒ Central Park has an interesting history.

15 Based on the map, what do you know about Central Park?

Ⓐ It has beautiful trees.

Ⓑ It is a national landmark.

Ⓒ It covers many city blocks.

Read "The Four Friends" before you answer Numbers 1 through 8.

The Four Friends

Four animals lived in a forest. They were the best of friends, but they were hungry. Food was a **valuable** thing in the forest. It had great worth.

The friends had a good idea. They wanted to grow a fruit tree that would give them food.

Monkey asked, "Where can we plant it? How can we find a spot?"

Rabbit said, "Don't worry. I can hop around to look."

Rabbit soon hopped back. She led her friends to a clear spot in the forest that was filled with sunlight.

Then, Rabbit asked, "How will we find a seed?"

Bird said, "Don't worry. I can fly around and find one."

Bird found a seed deep in the forest. The friends planted it. Then Bird said, "We need to water it. How will we carry the water?"

Elephant said, "Don't worry. I can help."

Elephant went to a stream and filled his trunk with water. Then, he watered the tree every day.

The tree grew and grew. Finally, the friends saw the first fruit! It was the **moment** they had been waiting for. In that second, they ate the fruit and they were no longer hungry.

When the tree grew tall, the friends could not reach the fruit. This was Monkey's chance to help. He said, "I will climb the tree and bring the fruit to you."

The four friends worked together. Through **cooperation**, they were able to grow plenty of fruit. In this way, the friends made a source of food. They saved some seeds from the fruit they ate. Then they planted more trees. Now, they have food for all the animals in the forest.

GO ON →

Name: _____ Date: _____

Use "The Four Friends" to answer Numbers 1 through 8.

1 Who is telling this story?

Ⓐ Monkey

Ⓑ Elephant

Ⓒ a narrator not in the story

2 Which BEST explains what the friends want to do in the story?

Ⓐ They want to have enough food to eat.

Ⓑ They want to grow a forest for the animals.

Ⓒ They want to help animals around the world.

3 Read this sentence from the story.

> **Food was a valuable thing in the forest.**

Which clue word in the story helps to explain what *valuable* means?

Ⓐ best

Ⓑ hungry

Ⓒ worth

GO ON →

Unit Assessment • Unit 2   Grade 3   133

Name: _____ Date: _____

4 Which sentence from the text BEST supports the story's message?

Ⓐ Four animals lived in a forest.

Ⓑ Then, Rabbit asked, "How will we find a seed?"

Ⓒ In this way, the friends made a source of food.

5 Read these sentences from the story.

It was the moment they had been waiting for. In that second, they ate the fruit and they were no longer hungry.

Which word in these sentences means almost the SAME as *moment*?

Ⓐ waiting

Ⓑ second

Ⓒ fruit

6 Why does Monkey decide to climb the tree?

Ⓐ He wants to run away.

Ⓑ He wants to feel important.

Ⓒ He wants to help his friends.

GO ON →

Name: _____ Date: _____

7 Read this sentence from the story.

> **Through cooperation, they were able to grow plenty of fruit.**

Which words from the story help to explain what *cooperation* means?

Ⓐ four friends

Ⓑ worked together

Ⓒ more trees

8 What is the lesson of the story?

Ⓐ Friends get things done together.

Ⓑ Always be kind to your friends.

Ⓒ It is easy to make new friends.

GO ON →

Read "Dolphins Work Together" before you answer Numbers 9 through 15.

Dolphins Work Together

Dolphins are smart animals. They show this in many ways. Dolphins talk to each other. They use clicks and squeaks. People have shown dolphins what they look like in a mirror. Some **recognized** themselves! They knew what they were looking at.

Dolphins show they are smart in another way: they work together to find food.

People have studied bottlenose dolphins near Florida. These dolphins hunt very fast fish. It is hard to catch the fish by chasing them. So, the dolphins hunt them in a different way.

First, the dolphins find the fish. They look in shallow water. One dolphin swims away from the group. It swims in wide circles. The dolphin swims around the fish. As it swims, it beats its tail. This brings up sand. The sand makes thick clouds. They confuse the fish.

The fish try to get away, but the dolphin keeps swimming. It swims in smaller circles. The clouds close around the fish. Soon, the fish are trapped.

GO ON →

Equator

Where Bottlenose Dolphins Live

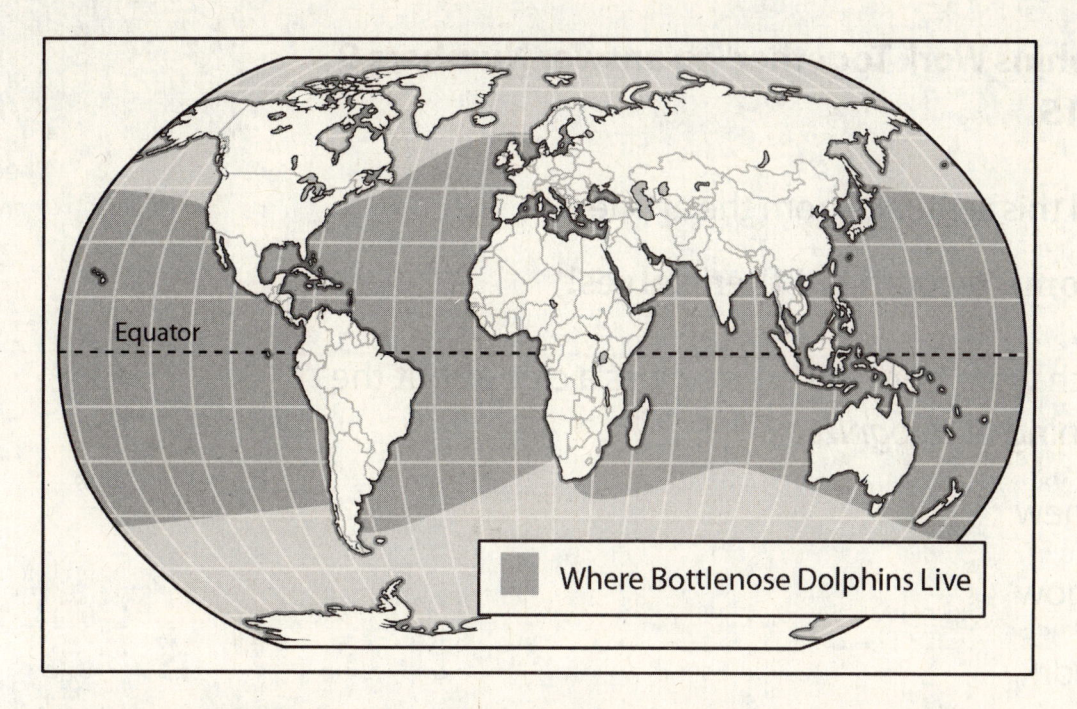

Bottlenose dolphins live all over the world. But only bottlenose dolphins in Florida use sand clouds to hunt fish.

The other dolphins come closer. They make sure the fish do not get away. The fish may jump out of the water. But the dolphins stick their heads up. When the fish jump, the dolphins catch them in their mouths! The dolphins work well together. They increase their chance of **success**.

This is just one way that dolphins work together. There are many others. People can learn a lot from dolphins. We should keep studying them. We will learn why dolphins work together. We might learn how people can work together, too.

GO ON →

Name: _____   Date: _____

Use "Dolphins Work Together" to answer Numbers 9 through 15.

9 Read this sentence from the article.

> **Some recognized themselves!**

Which word from the article gives a clue about the meaning of *recognized*?

Ⓐ knew

Ⓑ show

Ⓒ work

10 What is the author's point of view at the BEGINNING of the article?

Ⓐ People are very smart.

Ⓑ Dolphins are very smart.

Ⓒ Dolphins are smarter than people.

11 Which is NOT a detail that supports the author's point of view about dolphins?

Ⓐ Dolphins work together to find food.

Ⓑ People have studied bottlenose dolphins.

Ⓒ Dolphins talk to each other with different noises.

GO ON →

138   Grade 3

Unit Assessment • Unit 2

Name: _____ Date: _____

12 What information does the map show?

Ⓐ where dolphins hunt fish

Ⓑ where sand clouds are found

Ⓒ where to find bottlenose dolphins

13 Which words in the article show what *success* means?

Ⓐ work well together

Ⓑ their chance of

Ⓒ just one way

14 What point of view does the author have at the END of the article?

Ⓐ People should try to teach dolphins.

Ⓑ Dolphins do not always work together.

Ⓒ People should continue to study dolphins.

15 What does the author think people can learn from dolphins?

Ⓐ They can learn how to speak to dolphins.

Ⓑ They can learn how dolphins work together.

Ⓒ They can learn how different animals get along.

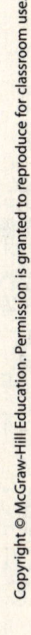

STOP

Unit Assessment • Unit 2

UNIT 3 UNIT

Read "Missing Mom and Dad" before you answer Numbers 1 through 7.

Missing Mom and Dad

The year was 1943. It was a hard time for people all over the world because of a war. Dad was a sailor in the U.S. Navy. Tara missed him because he was not living at home. He was on a ship at sea.

Tara lived with Mom and Tara's grandmother, Nana. They read Dad's letters together. This helped Tara miss Dad a little less. They also listened to news about the war on the radio. Sometimes, Tara felt afraid for the sailors and soldiers. She thought about the **bravery** they needed to defend their country.

One day after school, Mom had good news. Nana turned off the radio. Mom smiled and looked excited. "I want to do more to help our country. I also want to help our family. So I got a job," Mom said.

Tara looked at Mom in **dismay**. She was surprised and upset. Dad was already away from home. Now Mom would be away most of the day, too. This was not good news at all!

Mom explained that she was going to build ships for the navy. "Sailors like Dad will live and work on these ships," Mom said.

"Who will take care of me and Nana?" Tara asked. "Who will eat dinner with us?"

GO ON →

Name: _____ Date: _____

"You and Nana can take care of each other," Mom said. "I'll be home in time for dinner every night."

Tara felt sad because she missed Mom already. She ran to her room.

Moments later, Nana came to see her. "I'm happy your mom can help our family," Nana said. "She will do important work. You should be proud of her."

Weeks later, Nana read a letter that had come. Dad wrote that he missed his family very much. But he felt happy and proud because Mom got the job. "One of the ships Mom builds will get me home safely," he wrote.

Tara pictured Dad coming home on this ship. As a result, she started to feel better. She went downstairs to tell Mom she was proud of her, too.

Use "Missing Mom and Dad" to answer Numbers 1 through 7.

1. Why is it a hard time in the world when this story takes place?

   Ⓐ Dad is in the U.S. Navy.

   Ⓑ There is a war going on.

   Ⓒ The news is on the radio.

Unit Assessment • Unit 3

GO ON ➔

Grade 3 141

Name: _____ Date: _____

2 What problem does Tara have at the BEGINNING of the story?

Ⓐ She misses Dad while he is away.

Ⓑ She does not want to build navy ships.

Ⓒ She thinks they will not have enough money.

3 How does Tara's family help her solve this problem?

Ⓐ They listen to music on the radio.

Ⓑ They read Dad's letters together.

Ⓒ Mom gets a job building ships.

4 Read these sentences from the story.

> **Sometimes, Tara felt afraid for the sailors and soldiers. She thought about the bravery they needed to defend their country.**

Which word from these sentences means almost the OPPOSITE of *bravery*?

Ⓐ afraid

Ⓑ thought

Ⓒ defend

GO ON →

142 Grade 3 Unit Assessment • Unit 3

5 Why does Mom get a job?

Ⓐ She wants to tell Tara and Nana some good news.

Ⓑ She wants to help her country and her family.

Ⓒ She wants to build ships for Tara's dad.

6 Read this sentence from the story.

Tara looked at Mom in dismay.

Which sentence from the story helps you know what *dismay* means?

Ⓐ Mom smiled and looked excited.

Ⓑ "I also want to help our family."

Ⓒ She was surprised and upset.

7 How does Tara's family help her solve her problem at the END of the story?

Ⓐ Nana and Tara get closer while Mom works.

Ⓑ Mom's new job gives Tara time to herself.

Ⓒ Nana talks to Tara and reads Dad's letter.

GO ON →

Read "The Hoover Dam" before you answer Numbers 8 through 15.

The Hoover Dam

The Southwest is sunny and warm. States like California and Arizona are in this part of the U.S. In the 1930s, many Americans were moving there. People thought it was a nice place to live. Cities and towns grew. The Hoover Dam helped to make this possible.

A dam is something people build to hold back water. The Hoover Dam was built on the Colorado River. People started building it in 1931. It took five years to finish. The dam is very big. It was the biggest dam in the world at that time.

People built the dam on hard rock. First, they made a dry place on the river. They used tunnels to do this. Next, they dug out the soft mud on the river floor. Then they started to build. They used a **material** called concrete. The dam is made with enough concrete for a road 4,000 miles long!

The Southwest is dry. Much of it is desert. With more people, more water was needed. The Hoover Dam created a large lake. It was able to supply homes with water. Farmers needed to grow more food to feed more people. They needed more water to do this. The lake could **support** bigger farms by providing water.

GO ON →

Before the Hoover Dam was built, the Colorado River flooded each spring. The floods ruined farms. The dam also solved this problem for farmers.

As towns and cities grew, businesses also **boomed**. They needed a cheap source of power. The Hoover Dam uses power from the river to make electricity. It is still a big source of power today.

Homes and farms need water. Businesses need cheap power. The Hoover Dam gives these things. It has helped a big part of our country to grow.

Today, the Hoover Dam sends electricity to areas in the Southwest. Arizona, Nevada, and the city of Los Angeles use about 57% of this power.

Who Uses Electricity from the Hoover Dam?

Arizona	Los Angeles	Nevada
19%	15%	23%

GO ON →

Name: _____ Date: _____

Use "The Hoover Dam" to answer Numbers 8 through 15.

8 What is the MAIN idea of the first paragraph?

Ⓐ Towns and cities grew in the Southwest in the 1930s.

Ⓑ California and Arizona are states in the Southwest.

Ⓒ The Southwest can be a very nice place to live.

9 What did workers do RIGHT AFTER they made a dry place for the dam on the river?

Ⓐ They started to build the dam.

Ⓑ They made tunnels under the ground.

Ⓒ They dug out the soft mud from the river floor.

10 Read this sentence from the article.

They used a material called concrete.

Which words from the article help you understand what *material* means?

Ⓐ is made with

Ⓑ was needed

Ⓒ grow more

GO ON →

146   Grade 3   Unit Assessment • Unit 3

Name: _____ Date: _____

11 What happened BEFORE the Hoover Dam was built?

Ⓐ Businesses easily got cheap power.

Ⓑ The Colorado River flooded and ruined farms.

Ⓒ Homes and farms in the area got plenty of water.

12 Read these sentences from the article.

> **They needed more water to do this. The lake could support bigger farms by providing water.**

Which words from these sentences help you understand the meaning of *support*?

Ⓐ to do

Ⓑ the lake

Ⓒ providing water

13 According to the chart, how much electricity from the Hoover Dam does Arizona use?

Ⓐ 15%

Ⓑ 19%

Ⓒ 23%

GO ON →

Name: _____ Date: _____

14 Read these sentences from the article.

> **As towns and cities grew, businesses also boomed. They needed a cheap source of power.**

Which word from the sentences helps you understand the meaning of *boomed*?

Ⓐ grew

Ⓑ source

Ⓒ power

15 Based on the key details, what is the MAIN idea of the article?

Ⓐ The Hoover Dam was built along the Colorado River.

Ⓑ The Hoover Dam was the biggest dam in the world in the 1930s.

Ⓒ Power and water from the Hoover Dam helped the Southwest grow.

Read "Baker's Dozen" before you answer Numbers 1 through 8.

Baker's Dozen

In a small German town, there was once a baker named Hugo. He made the best cakes. He also made the most delicious cookies in town.

One evening, Hugo was closing his bakery. Suddenly an old woman walked in. The woman had white hair and long, boney fingers. She wore a long black coat that was full of holes.

Hugo was upset because this woman had **interrupted** his work. He had been in the middle of cleaning up when she came and stopped him.

"Can I help you?" Hugo asked with a frown.

"Yes, please. May I have a dozen cookies?" the old woman asked.

The woman said many kind words to the baker.

"How I love your bakery!" she said. "The smell of baked bread fills the shop in such a delicious way."

But the baker said nothing. He shoved the box of cookies at her.

"May I have one more cookie for my cold walk home?" the old woman asked.

"No, you may not!" Hugo snapped back. "You have your twelve cookies. Now please leave!"

The old woman apologized and quietly left.

Over the next few days, Hugo realized that few customers were coming to his bakery. He also found that his treats no longer tasted good. He made a **variety** of cakes and cookies. But all of them were terrible.

Then on a rainy night, when Hugo was very upset, the old lady returned.

"Is everything okay?" she asked.

"No, it is not," Hugo explained. "I have been having very bad luck. My bakery is ruined."

"I am sorry to hear that. But maybe you should be nicer to your customers," the woman said.

Hugo **realized** that his behavior had been bad in the past. He knew that he had made a mistake.

"You are right," he said. "I was mean to you. I am sorry. Would you like another dozen cookies? I will always add one more cookie to the dozen. It will show that I am thankful to my nice customers."

"Thank you," said the old woman. "I'm sure your luck will improve soon."

Name: _____ Date: _____

Use "Baker's Dozen" to answer Numbers 1 through 8.

1 Who is telling the story?

Ⓐ Hugo

Ⓑ the old woman

Ⓒ a narrator not in the story

2 What does Hugo think of the old woman at the BEGINNING of the story?

Ⓐ She is very kind.

Ⓑ She should leave.

Ⓒ She can help him.

3 Which sentence from the story BEST helps you understand the meaning of *interrupted*?

Ⓐ She wore a long black coat that was full of holes.

Ⓑ He had been in the middle of cleaning up when she came and stopped him.

Ⓒ The woman said many kind words to the baker.

GO ON →

Unit Assessment • Unit 4   Grade 3   151

Name: _____ Date: _____

4 Read these sentences from the story.

> He made a variety of cakes and cookies.
> But all of them were terrible.

Which word from the sentences helps you know the meaning of *variety*?

Ⓐ made

Ⓑ cakes

Ⓒ all

5 What does Hugo think about the woman at the END of the story?

Ⓐ She is wise.

Ⓑ She is greedy.

Ⓒ She is strange.

6 Read this paragraph from the story.

> Hugo realized that his behavior had been bad in the past. He knew that he had made a mistake.

Which word from the paragraph means almost the SAME as *realized*?

Ⓐ been

Ⓑ knew

Ⓒ made

7 What lesson does Hugo learn from the old woman?

Ⓐ Always be kind to others.

Ⓑ Work hard for what you want.

Ⓒ Do not try to be something you are not.

8 What is a theme of this story?

Ⓐ Nothing is ever free.

Ⓑ Always try your best.

Ⓒ Bad actions have bad results.

GO ON →

Unit Assessment • Unit 4

Grade 3   153

Read "Flying Like Animals" before you answer Numbers 9 through 15.

Flying Like Animals

People fly in airplanes. Plane inventors used birds for inspiration. People fly in other ways, too. We use gliders, parachutes, and balloons. These tools help us soar through the sky in the same ways that some animals do.

Gliders

The flying fish is a **graceful** glider. It moves smoothly through the air. This is a very beautiful fish. It has long fins at its side. The fish jumps out of the water. It uses its fins like wings to soar. Its thin fins rest on the air. Then, it dives back underwater.

People use gliders to fly. Gliders look like the fins of the flying fish. People hold onto the gliders. They can soar through the sky. Gliders rest on the air like the fins of a flying fish.

Parachutes

There is a frog called the parachute frog. It uses a flap of skin between its toes. When it jumps from a high tree branch, the flap catches the wind. This slows the frog's fall. It can land safely on the ground.

The parachute frog is like a flying squirrel. The flying squirrel also uses a parachute. It has skin that connects all of its paws.

GO ON →

Humans make their own parachutes. They use parachutes to jump out of planes. The parachutes help them drop gently to the ground.

Ballooning

Small spiders use the wind to travel. They use the silk from their webs. The silk catches a breeze. This carries the spiders far away.

Hot-air balloons fly the same way. They use the wind and the balloon to carry them.

Animals can be very inspiring. Our flying tools are **related** to animals. They are similar. We can learn a lot from animals. We can even learn to fly!

Use "Flying Like Animals" to answer Numbers 9 through 15.

9 Read this sentence from the article.

> **The flying fish is a graceful glider.**

Which phrase from the article means about the SAME as *graceful*?

Ⓐ moves smoothly

Ⓑ through the air

Ⓒ has long fins

Name: _____ Date: _____

10 How are gliders and the fins of a flying fish ALIKE?

Ⓐ Both rest on the air.

Ⓑ Both are used in the ocean.

Ⓒ Both are made of the same material.

11 How are a parachute frog and a flying squirrel the SAME?

Ⓐ Both can fly from tree to tree.

Ⓑ Both have extra skin on their bodies.

Ⓒ Both use parachutes that humans made.

12 Why do people use parachutes?

Ⓐ to be safe

Ⓑ to fly in planes

Ⓒ to act like animals

GO ON →

Name: _____ Date: _____

13 According to the article, how do small spiders use the wind to travel?

Ⓐ The wind makes a web for them to walk along.

Ⓑ The wind lifts their bodies high off the ground.

Ⓒ The wind carries their webs to new places.

14 How are hot-air balloons and small spiders the SAME?

Ⓐ They both use the wind.

Ⓑ They both use silk from webs.

Ⓒ They both use a type of basket.

15 Read these sentences from the article.

> **Animals can be very inspiring. Our flying tools are related to animals. They are similar.**

Which word from the sentences helps you know what *related* means?

Ⓐ inspiring

Ⓑ flying

Ⓒ similar

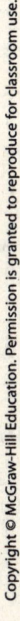

Unit Assessment • Unit 4 Grade 3 **157**

UNIT 5

Read "Frankie's New Doghouse" before you answer Numbers 1 through 8.

Frankie's New Doghouse

It was a sunny afternoon. Rachel was excited to play with her dog, Frankie. The golden retriever ran into the backyard. He jumped and barked in the fresh air. Poor Frankie had been cooped up in the house!

Rachel's mom was already in the backyard. She was wearing gloves and goggles. Her mom was really good at building and repairing things. Last year, they planted a big garden. Rachel wondered what new project she was working on, so she asked.

"I finally decided to **replace** this old tool shed. I'm going to build a new one," her mom said.

Rachel looked at the tool shed. It was made of wood. It was also chipped in places. The shed was not very big. It was only slightly taller than Frankie.

"What will you do with the old one?" asked Rachel.

"That's the problem. I'm not sure what to do with it, but I don't want to throw it away," said her mom.

Rachel had a sudden idea. The old shed could be turned into a doghouse. It would take some work, but Rachel thought it would be fun, too.

GO ON →

Her mother **considered** the idea. She needed to think about it before she agreed to the plan. She knew Frankie would love a doghouse. She also believed that **recycling** was important. A doghouse would be the perfect way to make something old new again. It would also give Rachel a fun project to do.

"I think it's a great idea," said her mom finally. "Let's gather the supplies together."

They got right to work. Rachel's mom used a saw to cut a dog door in the old shed. She helped Rachel sand the wood until it was smooth. After that, they painted the new doghouse bright blue. Rachel wrote Frankie's name in white paint over the door. Finally, they laid some old, soft blankets on the floor of the shelter.

When Frankie saw the doghouse, his tail wagged extra fast. He ran right inside and sat down.

"I think he likes it!" said Rachel with a laugh.

"And even better, we turned that old tool shed into something useful," said her mom.

Name: _____ Date: _____

Use "Frankie's New Doghouse" to answer Numbers 1 through 8.

1 What does Rachel think about the weather at the BEGINNING of the story?

Ⓐ It is good weather to build something new.

Ⓑ It is good weather for the dog to run outside.

Ⓒ It is good weather to do some gardening with her mom.

2 Why does Rachel ask her mom what she is doing in the backyard?

Ⓐ She wants to know what her mom is working on.

Ⓑ She wants to help her mom build a tool shed.

Ⓒ She wants to learn how to make a doghouse.

3 Which sentence in the story helps you figure out what *replace* means?

Ⓐ Her mom was really good at building and repairing things.

Ⓑ "I'm going to build a new one," her mom said.

Ⓒ "I'm not sure what to do with it, but I don't want to throw it away," said her mom.

GO ON →

160   Grade 3

Unit Assessment • Unit 5

Name: _____ Date: _____

4 What does Rachel think about creating a new doghouse?

Ⓐ She thinks it would be fun.

Ⓑ She thinks Frankie would love it.

Ⓒ She thinks recycling is important.

5 Read these sentences from the story.

> Her mother considered the idea. She needed to think about it before she agreed to the plan.

Which clue words in the sentence help to explain what *considered* means?

Ⓐ the idea

Ⓑ needed to think

Ⓒ agreed to the plan

6 Read this sentence from the story.

> She also believed that recycling was important.

Which words in the story help you figure out what *recycling* means?

Ⓐ would love a doghouse

Ⓑ would be the perfect way

Ⓒ make something old new again

GO ON →

Name: _____ Date: _____

7 What does Rachel think about the doghouse when it is done?

Ⓐ It is something that Frankie will like.

Ⓑ It was more work than she thought it would be.

Ⓒ It can be used in many different ways in the future.

8 What does Rachel's mom say that shows what she thinks about recycling?

Ⓐ "That's the problem."

Ⓑ "Let's gather the supplies together."

Ⓒ "And even better, we turned that old tool shed into something useful."

GO ON →

Read "Helicopter Rescue Swimmers" before you answer Numbers 9 through 15.

Helicopter Rescue Swimmers

Have you ever seen pictures of a storm at sea? They can cause big waves. This can be risky for people on ships. Hurricanes and other **disasters** can harm boats. They can strand people on cliffs. It takes a special team to save lives at sea. Helicopter rescue swimmers are part of that team.

These swimmers are part of the Coast Guard. The Coast Guard is part of our military. The Coast Guard gets a message when there is an emergency at sea. A helicopter is sent to help. The team on board works together to save lives.

Pilots have to be careful. Flying close to rough waves is tricky. When they are close enough, the team gets to work. One member will lower a rescue basket. Sometimes the rescue swimmer is inside. Other times, a rescue swimmer will jump from the helicopter.

It takes a lot of training to save lives at sea. Rescue swimmers go to a special school. They learn to swim in very cold water. They wear a special suit for this. They use SCUBA gear. They also learn to swim in big waves. As a result, rescue swimmers are very strong.

UNIT 5

In 1991, the Coast Guard in San Francisco got a call. Two boys were stuck in a cave. Helicopter Rescue swimmer Steve Frye was ready. He had trouble swimming in the tide. The waves were big and strong. But he kept swimming until he reached the cave. He did not **waver** from his task. He could only carry one boy at a time. So, Steve Frye had to swim into the cave twice! Because of his hard work, Frye was able to save lives.

It is very hard to become a rescue swimmer. Many people think the training is too much work. Rescue swimmers work hard all year. They have to stay healthy and strong. But rescue swimmers are an important part of the Coast Guard. They are always there to keep people safe at sea.

School for Helicopter Rescue Swimmers

Graduation Year	Number of Students
1984	2
2012	17

GO ON →

Name: _____ Date: _____

Use "Helicopter Rescue Swimmers" to answer Numbers 9 through 15.

9 Which word from the article is an example of a disaster?

  Ⓐ hurricanes

  Ⓑ harms

  Ⓒ boats

10 Read these sentences from the article.

  Pilots have to be careful. Flying close to rough waves is tricky.

  What does the author MOST LIKELY think about helicopter pilots?

  Ⓐ They must have a lot of skill.

  Ⓑ They should not fly over the sea.

  Ⓒ They should be in the Coast Guard.

11 Why are rescue swimmers very strong?

  Ⓐ They use SCUBA gear.

  Ⓑ They swim in very cold water.

  Ⓒ They learn to swim in big waves.

GO ON →

Unit Assessment • Unit 5   Grade 3   **165**

Name: _____ **Date:** _____

12 Which words from the article are almost the OPPOSITE of what *waver* means?

Ⓐ big and strong

Ⓑ kept swimming

Ⓒ carry one boy

13 Why was Steve Frye able to save the boys' lives?

Ⓐ He was an excellent helicopter pilot.

Ⓑ He knew the tide was too strong to swim in.

Ⓒ He worked very hard to become a rescue swimmer.

14 Which sentence from the text shows what the author thinks about helicopter rescue swimmers?

Ⓐ This can be risky for people on ships.

Ⓑ Many people think the training is too much work.

Ⓒ They are always there to keep people safe at sea.

15 Which conclusion can be made about the information in the chart?

Ⓐ More people are starting to become rescue swimmers.

Ⓑ Today, not as many rescue swimmers are needed.

Ⓒ It is getting harder to become a rescue swimmer.

STOP

Read "The Columbus Day Storm" before you answer Numbers 1 through 7.

The Columbus Day Storm

It was Columbus Day in 1962. At school in Oregon, I learned about the explorer Christopher Columbus. But I was having a hard time paying attention. Today was also Dad's birthday. I was thinking about making Dad's birthday special. After school, my little sister, Trish, and I were getting a birthday cake.

Someone shouted to me, "Look out the window, Billy!" Outside, the weather looked bad. There were storm clouds in the sky. They looked green and yellow and dark. I'd never seen clouds like that before. The wind was blowing hard. Trees were bending and branches broke off in the wind.

"Students, please stay in your seats." Mrs. Hoy sounded nervous. "The **forecast** didn't say there was going to be a bad storm."

The windstorm got worse, so Dad picked us up at school. There were fallen trees and power lines in the street. I became **alarmed** and afraid on the drive home.

"Are we going to get Dad's birthday cake?" Trish asked. I think she was too young to understand how dangerous the storm was.

"All I want for my birthday is for us to be safely together," Dad said. As we drove through town, I saw that the stores were already closed.

Name: _____ Date: _____

At home, Trish wanted to go outside and play. Dad picked her up in his arms. "This is a **serious** storm. It's no time for playing outside. We have to stay inside to stay safe," Dad said.

Later, the house lost power, but Dad was prepared with flashlights, batteries, and a radio. We listened to a news report. The winds were more than 100 miles per hour. "This is the most powerful storm to hit Oregon this century!" said a reporter.

The morning after the storm, Dad cooked breakfast in the fireplace. Trish and I still had to stay inside. There were fallen power lines, broken glass, and other dangers outside. We gave Dad birthday cards, and I told Dad I was sorry he didn't get cake on his birthday.

Dad smiled. "We were together and safe on my birthday," he said. "I couldn't ask for anything more."

Use "The Columbus Day Storm" to answer Numbers 1 through 7.

1 Who is telling this story?

Ⓐ Billy

Ⓑ Dad

Ⓒ Trish

Name: _____ Date: _____

2 Which words from the story help you know what *forecast* means?

Ⓐ never seen clouds like that before

Ⓑ sounded nervous

Ⓒ say there was going to be

3 Read these sentences from story.

> There were fallen trees and power lines in the street. I became alarmed and afraid on the drive home.

Which clue word in the sentences means almost the SAME as *alarmed*?

Ⓐ fallen

Ⓑ power

Ⓒ afraid

4 Which sentence shows what Billy thinks when Trish asks if they are going to get Dad's birthday cake?

Ⓐ I was thinking about making Dad's birthday special.

Ⓑ I think she was too young to understand how dangerous the storm was.

Ⓒ As we drove through town, I saw that the stores were already closed.

GO ON →

Unit Assessment • Unit 6   Grade 3   **169**

Name: _____ Date: _____

5 What does Dad want for his birthday?

  Ⓐ to be safe and with his kids

  Ⓑ to be prepared for the storm

  Ⓒ to get flashlights, batteries, and a radio

6 Read this sentence from the story.

  "**This is a serious storm.**"

  Which clue word in the story means almost the OPPOSITE of *serious*?

  Ⓐ outside

  Ⓑ playing

  Ⓒ prepared

7 What is the lesson of the story?

  Ⓐ Stay calm in emergency situations.

  Ⓑ It is important to be prepared for storms.

  Ⓒ Being safe with people you care about matters most.

GO ON →

Read "Cheetahs and Lions" before you answer Numbers 8 through 15.

Cheetahs and Lions

Cheetahs are big cats. Lions are also big cats. Both live in Africa. Sadly, both are also **endangered**. Not many live in the wild. People need to protect them or there may not be any cheetahs or lions left.

Cheetahs usually live alone. Cheetahs that are brothers may live together. But a female cheetah takes care of her cubs by herself. The cubs leave their mother after about a year.

Lions live in big groups. These groups are called prides. In a pride, most adult lions are females. They are related. They take care of the cubs in a pride. There is usually one adult male in a pride, but there can be a few males. Only male lions have a thick mane of hair. The lions in a pride can be very playful.

Cheetahs are smaller than lions. They are the fastest animal on land. A cheetah can sprint 65 miles per hour. A lion is fast, but not as fast as a cheetah. Lions can run about 35 miles per hour.

Cheetahs and lions hunt different animals for food, called prey. Cheetahs hunt small animals. They use their speed to catch prey. Lions hunt bigger animals. They use their strength to overpower prey.

These cats are in danger. Both are hunted by people. One step to protect these cats is to make it **illegal** to hunt them. Many countries in Africa now have laws to protect them. Another step is to protect where the cats live. Wildlife reservations are one way to do this. They are areas where cheetahs and lions can live safely away from people.

Cheetahs and lions are great hunters. But they need to be protected from people. We cannot let these big cats disappear from the wild.

Cheetah

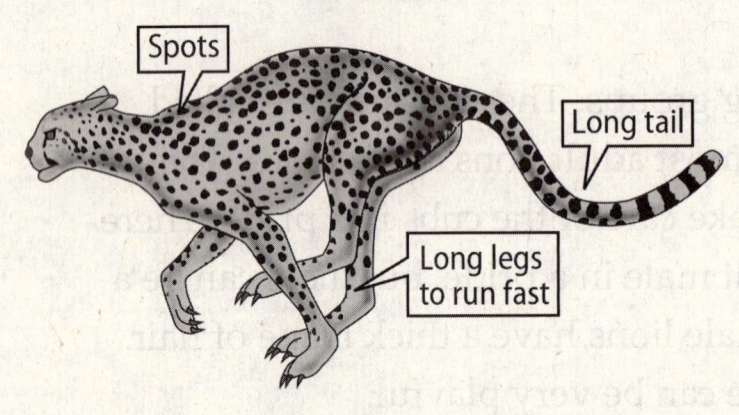

- Spots
- Long tail
- Long legs to run fast

Male Lion

- Mane
- Tail
- Legs

Name: _____ Date: _____

Use "Cheetahs and Lions" to answer Numbers 8 through 15.

8 How are cheetahs and lions ALIKE?

Ⓐ They are big cats that live in Africa.

Ⓑ They live in big groups called prides.

Ⓒ They leave their mothers when they are cubs.

9 Read this sentence from the article.

Sadly, both are also endangered.

Which sentence in the article helps you understand what *endangered* means?

Ⓐ Not many live in the wild.

Ⓑ A cheetah lives alone.

Ⓒ They are the fastest animal on land.

10 How are cheetahs and lions DIFFERENT?

Ⓐ Cheetahs are very fast, but lions cannot run at all.

Ⓑ Cheetahs take care of their cubs, but lions do not.

Ⓒ Cheetahs live alone, but lions live in big groups.

GO ON →

Unit Assessment • Unit 6 Grade 3 173

Name: _____ Date: _____

11 How do cheetahs hunt differently from lions?

Ⓐ Cheetahs sprint at 65 miles per hour to catch prey.

Ⓑ Cheetahs use their strength to overpower prey.

Ⓒ Cheetahs hunt bigger prey than lions do.

12 What problem does the author present in the article?

Ⓐ People hunt cheetahs and lions.

Ⓑ A lion is not as fast as a cheetah.

Ⓒ Cheetahs and lions must hunt for food.

13 Read these sentences from the article.

> One step to protect these cats is to make it illegal to hunt them. Many countries in Africa now have laws to protect them.

Which word from the sentences helps you understand the meaning of *illegal*?

Ⓐ step

Ⓑ countries

Ⓒ laws

GO ON →

174   Grade 3

Unit Assessment • Unit 6

Name: _____ Date: _____

14 Which sentence describes a way to solve the problem described in the article?

Ⓐ These cats are in danger.

Ⓑ Another step is to protect where the cats live.

Ⓒ We cannot let these big cats disappear from the wild.

15 According to the diagrams, what does a male lion have that cheetahs do not have?

Ⓐ a tail

Ⓑ a mane

Ⓒ long legs

Exit Assessment

Read "Fox Food" before you answer Numbers 1 through 8.

Fox Food

One day, Wes the fox went to play with his friends. He could not find them. He searched all over the forest. After a while, Wes became very hungry. He went back home to get something to eat, but there was no food!

"What is this? Why is there no food in the den?" Wes asked sadly. He could not hide his **disappointment**.

His grandma heard him. "Well, Wes," she said, "you have to find your own food. That is what all your friends are doing. They are out hunting for food."

Wes was upset. "It will not be easy to find food. I do not even know how!"

Grandma **encouraged** Wes to try. She pushed him to learn from the other forest animals. So, Wes went into the forest in search of food.

He soon found his pal Norman the rabbit. "How do you find food, Norman?" Wes asked.

"It is easy. I eat leaves from the plants and berries from the bushes. Here, try some of these," Norman said, handing Wes some berries.

"These are delicious!" Wes shouted.

GO ON →

Name: _____ Date: _____

Wes walked deeper into the forest to look for berries. Then he saw his friend, Maggie the sparrow, sitting on a tree branch.

"Maggie, what are you eating?" Wes asked.

"I am eating some seeds I found. I also have a nut that I found high up in the oak tree. Try it," Maggie said. She tossed the nut to Wes, and he ate it.

"This is very tasty," Wes said.

Wes went back out to gather up all of the nuts and berries that had fallen and **tumbled** to the ground. He took them home. Grandma said, "I am very happy that you can now find your own food."

Wes was happy, too. He was no longer hungry.

Use "Fox Food" to answer Numbers 1 through 8.

1. Read this paragraph from the story.

    "What is this? Why is there no food in the den?" Wes asked sadly. He could not hide his disappointment.

    Which word from the paragraph helps you understand the meaning of *disappointment*?

    Ⓐ food

    Ⓑ sadly

    Ⓒ hide

Exit Assessment • Unit 1

GO ON →

Grade 3   179

Name: _____ Date: _____

2 How does Wes feel at first about hunting for food?

Ⓐ curious

Ⓑ excited

Ⓒ unhappy

3 Read this sentence from the story.

Grandma encouraged Wes to try.

Which word from the story has almost the SAME meaning as *encouraged*?

Ⓐ pushed

Ⓑ went

Ⓒ found

4 What happens AFTER Wes goes out to find food?

Ⓐ He plays with his friends.

Ⓑ He finds Norman the rabbit.

Ⓒ He returns home to get food.

5 What does Wes do AFTER he finds his friend Maggie?

Ⓐ He eats a nut.

Ⓑ He speaks to Norman.

Ⓒ He walks into the forest.

GO ON →

180 Grade 3

Exit Assessment • Unit 1

Name: _____ Date: _____

6 What does Wes learn from Norman and Maggie?

Ⓐ how to cook dinner

Ⓑ how to find his own food

Ⓒ how to pull leaves from plants

7 Read this sentence from the story.

Wes went back out to gather up all of the nuts and berries that had fallen and tumbled to the ground.

Which word from the sentence has almost the SAME meaning as *tumbled*?

Ⓐ went

Ⓑ gather

Ⓒ fallen

8 How does Wes feel at the end of the story?

Ⓐ angry

Ⓑ hungry

Ⓒ proud

Exit Assessment • Unit 1

GO ON →

Grade 3   181

Read "Mark Twain and the Mississippi River" before you answer Numbers 9 through 15.

Mark Twain and the Mississippi River

Mark Twain is one of America's best writers. People still read many of his stories today. Mark Twain's real name is Samuel Clemens. Clemens called himself "Mark Twain" when he wrote stories.

Clemens had an interesting life. He worked on the Mississippi River. He was a steamboat captain. He often wrote about the river in his stories.

The Beginning

Samuel Clemens grew up on the Mississippi River. He saw many steamboats come into his town. The boats brought all sorts of exciting people there. Clemens had many jobs when he was young. He wanted to make money for his family. He started out working for newspapers. Then, he moved to other cities to find the right job. None of the jobs made him happy. Finally, he decided to work on a steamboat.

Life on the River

Clemens always dreamed of working on a steamboat. He started out by helping a captain. Clemens learned how the boat worked. Then, he became a captain. It took two years of **effort**. It was hard work!

GO ON →

Clemens wrote many letters to his family. He told his family he loved the great Mississippi River. Finally, he found a job he loved. And he was able to make money for his family. Life on the river was perfect.

Writing

Clemens was a steamboat captain for two years. The Mississippi River **inspired** him. It made him want to write. He wrote many stories about life on the river. He even got his writing name from working on the steamboat. "Mark Twain" was a term used to check how deep the river was. Mark Twain's most famous story is *The Adventures of Huckleberry Finn*. It is about two friends who travel down the Mississippi River.

Parts of a Steamboat

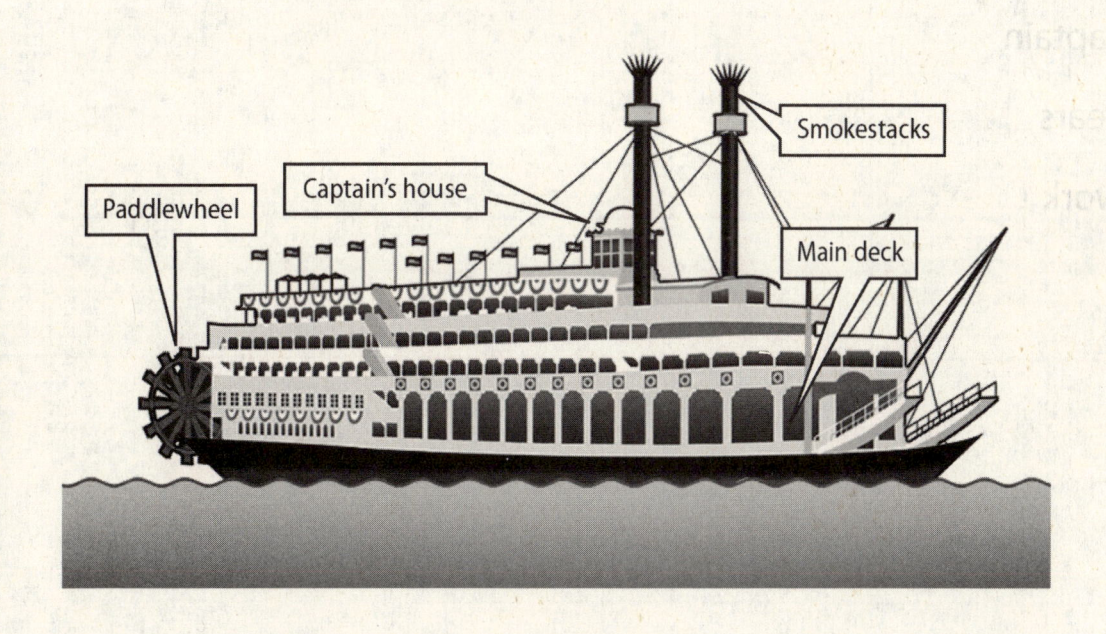

Name: _____ Date: _____

Use "Mark Twain and the Mississippi River" to answer Numbers 9 through 15.

9 What did Clemens do RIGHT BEFORE he became a steamboat captain?

Ⓐ He wrote stories about Huckleberry Finn.

Ⓑ He helped another captain of a steamboat.

Ⓒ He traveled to different cities looking for jobs.

10 Read these sentences from the article.

> **Then, he became a captain. It took two years of effort. It was hard work!**

Which word from these sentences has almost the SAME meaning as *effort*?

Ⓐ captain

Ⓑ years

Ⓒ work

GO ON →

Name: _____ Date: _____

11 What did Clemens tell his family in his letters to them?

　Ⓐ He said he wanted to come home.

　Ⓑ He said he loved the Mississippi River.

　Ⓒ He said he wanted to write for a newspaper.

12 How did Clemens get the name "Mark Twain"?

　Ⓐ from working on a steamboat

　Ⓑ from a character in a story

　Ⓒ from living in the city

13 Read this sentence from the article.

> **The Mississippi River inspired him.**

Which words from the article help to explain the meaning of *inspired*?

　Ⓐ was a steamboat captain

　Ⓑ made him want to

　Ⓒ check how deep

Exit Assessment • Unit 1

GO ON →

Grade 3

Name: _____ Date: _____

14 How did working on the Mississippi River affect Clemens?

Ⓐ He wrote about life on the river.

Ⓑ He went back to working for the newspaper.

Ⓒ He worked as a steamboat captain his whole life.

15 In the diagram of the steamboat, where is the captain's house where Clemens would stay as captain?

Ⓐ behind the paddlewheel

Ⓑ near the top of the boat

Ⓒ below the main deck

Read "Mateo's Voyage" before you answer Numbers 1 through 8.

Mateo's Voyage

It was the summer of 1492. Finally, there was some excitement in my boring town. Everyone was talking about Christopher Columbus. Columbus was a sea captain. He planned to sail to the distant lands of Japan, China, and India. There he would find **resources** like spices, silk, and other rare goods.

The King and Queen of Spain hoped Columbus could reach these lands by sea. That way, Spain could trade with them. Then they could sell the goods in Europe. Spain would become very rich.

Most importantly, Columbus was setting sail from my town, Palos. Palos is a town in Spain by the sea. My father was a fisherman there. I helped him catch fish and care for his boat.

I spent lots of time by the docks. The sailors told stories of their travels. They told about distant kingdoms. They told about strange plants and animals. I had lived in Palos my entire life. But I wanted to see more. I wanted to tell my own stories.

I had spent my whole life around ships. I knew I'd be useful. I had to find a way to sail with Columbus. But before I could go, I had to tell my parents.

Name: _____ Date: _____

When I **announced** my plans, Mother did not want me to go. She thought the voyage would be too dangerous. But Father understood. He had sailed with traders and merchants when he was young.

"Mateo is growing up," Father told Mother. "He is already a young man. He cannot stay in Palos his whole life. I felt the same when I was his age. He should get out and explore the world. Who knows what he will discover?"

Father was able to **convince** my mother. She agreed to let me go.

I could hardly believe my luck. I thanked them both. Then I set out for the docks. As I ran, I dreamed of the stories I would tell when I got home.

Use "Mateo's Voyage" to answer Numbers 1 through 8.

1 What are some examples of *resources* in the story?

Ⓐ spices and silk

Ⓑ Japan and China

Ⓒ the King and Queen

GO ON →

Name: _____ **Date:** _____

2 Why does Mateo want to sail with Columbus?

Ⓐ It will make him very rich.

Ⓑ He will get to see the world.

Ⓒ It will make his father happy.

3 What key detail supports Mateo's point of view about sailing?

Ⓐ The sailors tell stories about distant lands.

Ⓑ He had spent his whole life around ships.

Ⓒ His mother worries about him.

4 Read this sentence from the story.

> **When I announced my plans, Mother did not want me to go.**

Which sentence from the story helps to explain what *announced* means?

Ⓐ I had lived in Palos my entire life.

Ⓑ I wanted to tell my own stories.

Ⓒ But before I could go, I had to tell my parents.

GO ON →

Exit Assessment • Unit 2   Grade 3   189

Name: _____ Date: _____

5 What does Mateo's mother think about his voyage?

   Ⓐ It will be too dangerous for Mateo.

   Ⓑ Mateo's father needs his help at home.

   Ⓒ Mateo is too young to travel by himself.

6 Which word in the story gives a clue about the meaning of *convince*?

   Ⓐ explore

   Ⓑ discover

   Ⓒ agreed

7 Which detail about Mateo's father supports his point of view about his son?

   Ⓐ He lived in a Spanish town by the sea.

   Ⓑ He had sailed when he was young.

   Ⓒ He was a fisherman.

8 What is the theme of "Mateo's Voyage"?

   Ⓐ If you work hard, you will be rewarded.

   Ⓑ Young people should get out and explore the world.

   Ⓒ It is important for countries to trade with each other.

GO ON →

190　Grade 3　　　　　　　　　　　　　　　　Exit Assessment • Unit 2

Read "Velcro: A Sticky Solution" before you answer Numbers 9 through 15.

Velcro: A Sticky Solution

Great solutions can be found in nature. That is what we can learn from the **inventor**, or maker, of velcro!

Georges de Mestral was a Swiss engineer. Georges liked to look for new ways to solve problems. In 1941, he went for a walk in the woods. He took his dog. Georges found two burrs stuck to his pants. Burrs are small seeds with hooks. He looked at them under a microscope. Georges saw that the hooks attached to tiny loops on his pants. He had an idea.

Georges spent eight years researching. He worked hard. Then, he **created** two strips of fabric. He made them so that they attached the same way as burrs. One piece had thousands of tiny loops. The other piece had thousands of tiny hooks. He called this material "velcro." It combined the words "velvet" and "crochet."

Many people liked velcro. Georges sold more than sixty million yards a year!

Velcro is now used in many clothes. You may have shoes with velcro. You may have a jacket.

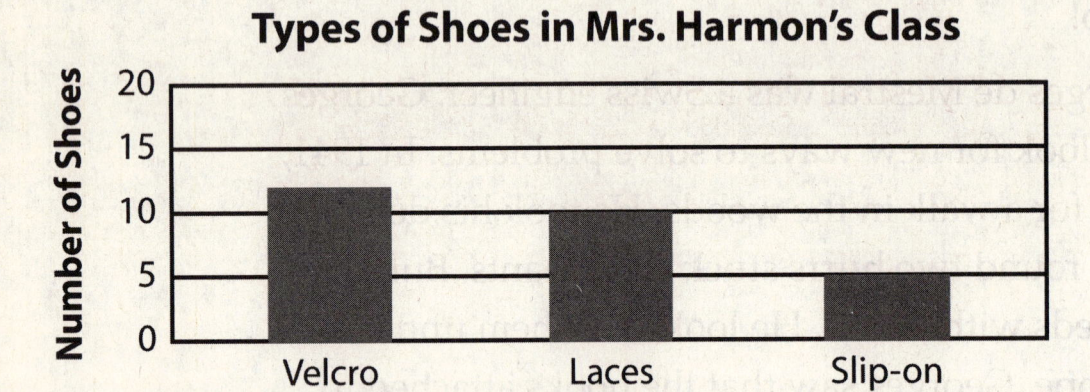

But you may be surprised at some of the ways it has been used! Velcro has been in space. It is used for astronaut suits. Velcro makes it easier for astronauts to get in and out of the suits. Velcro is also used by doctors. It holds equipment. Velcro helps in many ways!

Types of Shoes in Mrs. Harmon's Class

A bar graph showing Number of Shoes (0 to 20) by Type of Shoe:
- Velcro: 12
- Laces: 10
- Slip-on: 5

Name: _____ Date: _____

Use "Velcro: A Sticky Solution" to answer Numbers 9 through 15.

9 Read this paragraph from the article.

> Great solutions can be found in nature. That is what we can learn from the inventor, or maker, of velcro!

Which clue word in this paragraph restates what *inventor* means?

Ⓐ solutions

Ⓑ nature

Ⓒ maker

10 Read this sentence from the article.

> Georges liked to look for new ways to solve problems.

How does the author MOST LIKELY feel about Georges de Mestral?

Ⓐ He had a lot of ideas.

Ⓑ He gave up too easily.

Ⓒ He was fun to be around.

Exit Assessment • Unit 2

GO ON ➡

Grade 3

Name: _____   Date: _____

11 Read this sentence from the article.

> **Then, he created two strips of fabric.**

Which clue word in the article helps you figure out what *created* means?

Ⓐ spent

Ⓑ made

Ⓒ attached

12 With which statement would the author MOST LIKELY agree?

Ⓐ Velcro is not easy for everyone to use.

Ⓑ Georges de Mestral should have sold more velcro.

Ⓒ There are more uses for velcro than you might think.

13 Read this sentence from the article.

> **Velcro helps in many ways!**

What does the author think about velcro?

Ⓐ It is a good invention.

Ⓑ It is better than a zipper.

Ⓒ It is not as helpful as a button.

GO ON ➔

194   Grade 3   Exit Assessment • Unit 2

Name: _____ Date: _____

14 What does the author think about nature?

Ⓐ It is filled with man-made things.

Ⓑ It can help us solve problems.

Ⓒ It needs to be explored.

15 According to the bar graph, how many velcro shoes do students wear in Mrs. Harmon's class?

Ⓐ 5

Ⓑ 10

Ⓒ 12

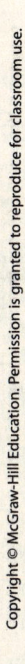

Exit Assessment • Unit 2 Grade 3 195

Read "Frog's Journey" before you answer Numbers 1 through 8.

Frog's Journey

Long ago, Frog lived in a lively stream in a place called Kyoto. Each day, Frog woke to feel the cool water on his smooth, green skin. He stretched his legs and leaped from stone to stone. There were plenty of lily pads to **appreciate**. He was happy to live in a place with so many of them. But Frog had never been anywhere else. This made him very sad.

One day, Goldfish swam up to Frog and asked what was wrong. Frog told him he wanted to see the world.

"Unlike me, you are a frog," said Goldfish. "You can leave the stream. You should visit Osaka! It has muddy ponds and green grass. It is very different from Kyoto."

Frog felt **nervous**, but he wanted to be brave. So off he went to Osaka. First, Frog hopped along a valley. Then, he climbed a mountain road. It took many days. Finally, he reached the top. Frog was very tired. He missed Kyoto. He wanted to go back.

That is when he spotted Toad. Toad was from Osaka.

"I'm on my way to Kyoto," said Toad. "I wanted to see the world. Traveling just makes me so tired!"

"We have the same problem," said Frog with a sigh.

GO ON →

Toad had an idea. If they were taller, they could see each other's homes from far away. First, they could take turns holding each other up high. Then, they could decide if they should finish their journeys.

But Frog and Toad were both missing home. So when Toad lifted Frog, Frog accidentally looked back at Kyoto.

"Why, Osaka looks just like Kyoto!" said Frog in **disbelief**. "It even has a lively stream. I can't believe the world is the same all over!"

When Frog held Toad up, Toad did the same thing. He was looking at Osaka, but thought he was seeing Kyoto.

"There's no need to travel. Our homes are the same!" said Toad.

So Frog and Toad said goodbye. Then they hopped back to their homes. They had not bothered to look very hard. So, they spent the rest of their days thinking the world was the same all over.

Name: _____ Date: _____

Use "Frog's Journey" to answer Numbers 1 through 8.

1 Read this sentence from the story.

> **There were plenty of lily pads to appreciate.**

Which word in the story helps you understand the meaning of *appreciate*?

Ⓐ cool

Ⓑ smooth

Ⓒ happy

2 What does Goldfish think Frog should do to solve his problem?

Ⓐ Frog should visit Osaka.

Ⓑ Frog should go find Toad.

Ⓒ Frog should climb a mountain.

3 Which word in the text means the OPPOSITE of *nervous*?

Ⓐ sad

Ⓑ different

Ⓒ brave

GO ON →

198 Grade 3

Exit Assessment • Unit 3

Name: _____ Date: _____

4 While on his journey, why does Frog want to go back to Kyoto?

Ⓐ He misses his home.

Ⓑ He is too tired to travel on.

Ⓒ He wants to tell Goldfish something.

5 What evidence from the text gives a clue about how Frog and Toad will solve their problem?

Ⓐ Frog sighed while he was talking.

Ⓑ Both Frog and Toad wanted to see the world.

Ⓒ Toad thought they could see each other's cities if they were taller.

6 Why do Frog and Toad think that the world is the same all over?

Ⓐ They see muddy ponds and lily pads every place they go.

Ⓑ They look at their own homes when they hold each other up.

Ⓒ They walk around the whole world together and see nothing new.

GO ON →

Exit Assessment • Unit 3   Grade 3   **199**

Name: _____ Date: _____

7 Which sentence from the story gives a clue to the meaning of *disbelief*?

Ⓐ "It even has a lively stream."

Ⓑ "I can't believe the world is the same all over!"

Ⓒ "Our homes are the same!"

8 Why do Frog and Toad say goodbye at the end of the story?

Ⓐ They decide to go home.

Ⓑ They do not like each other.

Ⓒ They want to find a new place to visit.

GO ON →

Read "Halley's Comet" before you answer Numbers 9 through 15.

Halley's Comet

Thousands of years ago, astronomers in China saw something amazing. A big ball of light with a long, bright tail appeared in the night sky. It was beautiful. They were looking at a comet.

A comet is made up of rocks and ice. It is often called a "dirty snowball." Planets in our solar system orbit the Sun. So do many comets. Comets sometimes get close to the Sun. The Sun's **warmth** heats the comet. This causes gas and dust to trail behind it. On Earth, this looks like a bright, white tail.

In 1682, a comet showed up in the sky. A man named Edmond Halley watched it. He wrote down what he saw. Halley loved astronomy. It was one reason he studied comets. Halley even read about comets that other people had seen. Two of these had **identical** orbits as the one he saw in 1682. Could it be the same one?

Halley wanted to find out. So, he studied the solar system. He met with his friend Isaac Newton. They talked about gravity. Gravity was a new idea at the time. He read more about the other two comets. Halley was sure they were the same one. He thought it orbited the Sun about every 76 years. Halley predicted the comet would be seen again in 1758.

UNIT 3
EXIT

By December of 1758, the comet had not been seen. It showed up just five days before the end of the year! Edmond Halley had been right. He did not live to see it, but other astronomers did. They named it Halley's Comet in his honor.

Today, we know the astronomers in China were looking at Halley's Comet all those years ago. About every 76 years, people get excited for the comet to return. The last time it was seen was in 1986. Spaceships around the world were ready for it. Halley's Comet was the first comet to be photographed from space. Keep your eyes open for Halley's Comet in 2061!

Famous Comets in our Solar System
Comet Hale Bopp was last seen in 1995.
Comet Shoemaker-Levy 9 was last seen in 1992.
Halley's Comet was last seen in 1986.

GO ON →

Name: _____ Date: _____

Use "Halley's Comet" to answer Numbers 9 through 15.

9 Read these sentences from the article.

> **Comets sometimes get close to the Sun.**
> **The Sun's warmth heats the comet.**

Which clue word from the sentences helps to explain what *warmth* means?

Ⓐ comets

Ⓑ close

Ⓒ heats

10 When was Halley's Comet FIRST seen?

Ⓐ 76 years ago

Ⓑ in December of 1758

Ⓒ thousands of years ago

11 Read this sentence from the article.

> **A comet is made up of rocks and ice.**

Which sentence from the text supports this idea?

Ⓐ It is often called a "dirty snowball."

Ⓑ Planets in our solar system orbit the Sun.

Ⓒ In 1682, a comet showed up in the sky.

GO ON →

Exit Assessment • Unit 3   Grade 3   203

Name: _____ Date: _____

12 Which event happened AFTER Halley's Comet was named for Edmond Halley?

Ⓐ Astronomers in China saw the comet.

Ⓑ Spaceships took photos of the comet.

Ⓒ Halley talked to Newton about the comet.

13 Which detail in the text helps to explain what *identical* means?

Ⓐ Halley loved astronomy.

Ⓑ Other people wrote about comets.

Ⓒ Halley thought the comets might be the same one.

14 What is the MAIN idea of the article?

Ⓐ Comets are made up of rocks and ice.

Ⓑ Halley's Comet has been seen throughout history.

Ⓒ Edmond Halley and Isaac Newton were astronomers.

15 Which statement is true based on the chart?

Ⓐ There are other comets in our solar system.

Ⓑ Halley's Comet is the most famous comet.

Ⓒ All comets have different orbits.

Read "Jane and the Flat Tire" before you answer Numbers 1 through 8.

Jane and the Flat Tire

"Can you take me to the mechanic shop?" Jane asked her dad. "I want to see Neil."

"Sure," her dad said, "but later Mrs. Howard is picking you up for your soccer game."

"Don't worry, I'll be ready," said Jane.

Jane's brother Neil is older and does not live at home anymore. He has his own house and an important job as a car mechanic. When cars break down, people bring them to Neil and he fixes them.

"Neil!" Jane shouted as she ran out of the car to hug her brother.

"Hi, Jane. Do you want to help me fix this car? It has a flat tire."

"I'd love to!" Jane said as they walked over to the car.

Neil **controlled** a machine in the garage. He handled the machine so that it slowly lifted the car. Then he showed Jane how to take off the broken tire and put on a new one. Jane tried to help, but it was hard work.

"How can you do this all day?" Jane asked.

"I love helping people," Neil explained, "and this is a useful skill to have."

GO ON →

UNIT 4
EXIT

Later, Mrs. Howard came to pick up Jane. As they drove to the soccer game, Jane told her friends all about her day with Neil. Suddenly, everyone heard a loud POP!

"Oh, no! I'm sorry, kids," Mrs. Howard **apologized**. "We must have a flat tire. It looks like we will be late to the game."

"I know how to fix it!" Jane said from the backseat. She showed Mrs. Howard everything her brother Neil had taught her. Together, they quickly fixed the tire. Soon, the car was back in **motion** and they were on their way to the game.

"Thank you so much for your help, Jane," Mrs. Howard said. "If it weren't for you, we never would have made it to the game on time."

"Don't thank me, Mrs. Howard. Thank my brother," Jane said with a smile.

GO ON →

Name: _____ Date: _____

Use "Jane and the Flat Tire" to answer Numbers 1 through 8.

1 What does Jane think of her older brother Neil?

Ⓐ She likes to visit him.

Ⓑ She wants him to live at home.

Ⓒ She wants him to come to her game.

2 Which sentence from the story shows what Jane thinks about helping Neil?

Ⓐ "Can you take me to the mechanic shop?" Jane asked her dad.

Ⓑ When cars break down, people bring them to Neil and he fixes them.

Ⓒ "I'd love to!" Jane said as they walked over to the car.

3 Read these sentences from the story.

> **Neil controlled a machine in the garage. He handled the machine so that it slowly lifted the car.**

Which word from the sentences has the SAME meaning as *controlled*?

Ⓐ handled

Ⓑ slowly

Ⓒ lifted

GO ON →

Exit Assessment • Unit 4   Grade 3   207

Name: _____ Date: _____

4 What lesson does Jane learn from her brother in this story?

Ⓐ It can be easy to fix things.

Ⓑ It is good to have a useful skill.

Ⓒ People do more when they work together.

5 Read this paragraph from the story.

> "Oh, no! I'm sorry, kids," Mrs. Howard apologized. "We must have a flat tire. It looks like we will be late to the game."

Which word from the paragraph helps you know the meaning of *apologized*?

Ⓐ sorry

Ⓑ tire

Ⓒ looks

6 What does Jane think about having a flat tire on the way to the game?

Ⓐ She can learn a new skill.

Ⓑ She can call her brother.

Ⓒ She can help fix the tire.

GO ON →

208 Grade 3   Exit Assessment • Unit 4

Name: _____   Date: _____

7 Read this sentence from the story.

> **Soon, the car was back in motion and they were on their way to the game.**

Which phrase from the sentence helps you know the meaning of *motion*?

Ⓐ the car was back

Ⓑ on their way

Ⓒ to the game

8 What is the theme of this story?

Ⓐ Learning a new skill is hard to do.

Ⓑ It is good to share the skills you have.

Ⓒ You must have skills to get where you want to go.

Exit Assessment • Unit 4

GO ON →

Grade 3   209

Read "The Bumblebee Bat" before you answer Numbers 9 through 15.

The Bumblebee Bat

There are many different bats in the world. Some have big ears for hearing. Others have long wings. One type of bat is the bumblebee bat. It is the size of a bumblebee. That is how it was given its name. This bat is very small. In fact it is the smallest mammal in the world. It weighs only as much as a dime!

Kitti's Hog-nosed Bat

The bumblebee bat is also called "Kitti's hog-nosed bat." Kitti is the name of the scientist who found the tiny bat. It is called a hog-nosed bat because it has a nose that looks like a pig nose.

Bumblebee bats live in Asia. The **environment** they live in is a lot like the homes of other bats. They live in warm locations. Bumblebee bats are found high up in dark caves. They usually live in small groups of around ten bats. **Adventurous** scientists have explored these caves. They have found large groups of up to 100 bats!

Getting Around

Bumblebee bats use sound to find their way around. They make noises. The noises bounce off the cave's walls. The echo tells them how far away the wall is. This is called *echolocation*. Many bats use it. It helps them fly in the dark.

GO ON →

Name: _____ Date: _____

Life in the Cave

Bumblebee bats mostly stay in their caves. The caves keep them safe. They only leave to hunt for insects. The bats hunt in the morning and at night. They hunt for about 30 minutes at a time. This is not as long as other bats hunt. These little bats do not need a lot of food since they have very small bellies.

Bumblebee bats are very interesting animals. They have adapted to their homes. They may be small, but bumblebee bats are very special!

Use "The Bumblebee Bat" to answer Numbers 9 through 15.

9 How did the bumblebee bat get its name?

Ⓐ from its small size

Ⓑ from the noises it makes

Ⓒ from the shape of its nose

10 What is the bumblebee bat's nose compared to in the article?

Ⓐ a dime

Ⓑ Kitti's nose

Ⓒ a pig's nose

Name: _____ Date: _____

11 Read these sentences from the article.

> **The environment they live in is a lot like the homes of other bats. They live in warm locations.**

Which word from the sentences does NOT have the same meaning as *environment*?

Ⓐ homes

Ⓑ warm

Ⓒ locations

12 What do bumblebee bats do to find their way in the dark?

Ⓐ They live in small groups of ten.

Ⓑ They fly high up into dark caves.

Ⓒ They make noises that bounce off walls.

GO ON →

212　Grade 3　　　　　　　　　　　　　　　　　Exit Assessment • Unit 4

Name: _____ **Date:** _____

13 Read this sentence from the article.

> **Adventurous scientists have explored these caves.**

Which word from the sentence BEST helps you know what *adventurous* means?

Ⓐ scientists

Ⓑ explored

Ⓒ caves

14 How are bumblebee bats DIFFERENT from other bats?

Ⓐ They hunt for short periods of time.

Ⓑ They eat many different foods.

Ⓒ They use echolocation.

15 Why do bumblebee bats mostly stay in their caves?

Ⓐ to be safe

Ⓑ to eat food

Ⓒ to get larger

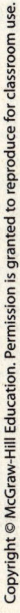

STOP

Exit Assessment • Unit 4   Grade 3   **213**

Read "Snake's Lesson" before you answer Numbers 1 through 8.

Snake's Lesson

Long ago, Dev the farmer planted seeds in his fields. He waited for them to grow. Weeks passed, but nothing happened. Dev did not understand what was wrong. How could he feed his family if the crops would not grow?

Just then, Snake came over. "What is wrong?" asked Snake. "You look very sad."

Dev told him about the trouble with his crops. Snake wanted to test Dev to see if he was a generous man.

"Bring me goat milk to drink. I will make sure your crops grow," said Snake.

Dev did not understand, but he did as he was told.

The next day, when Dev woke up he witnessed something **magnificent**! Crops had grown overnight. It was an amazing sight. Dev went to thank Snake by bringing more milk. He did this every day for years, and his fields were always full and healthy.

Raj was Dev's neighbor. Raj grew many good crops, but he was jealous of Dev. One day, he followed Dev and watched his neighbor give milk to Snake. So, he hurried to get his own milk to give to Snake.

"Why are you giving me milk?" asked Snake. "Your crops grow just fine."

"But they are not as fine as Dev's crops," replied Raj.

Snake was **horrified** to hear this. He was very upset that Raj was so greedy. Snake refused to help him, but Raj would not give up. He tried to capture Snake to make him help.

Snake was too fast and he got away, but he became angry. "Your crops will never grow again!" said Snake.

Dev heard what was happening and felt bad for Raj. He begged Snake not to hurt Raj's crops. Snake agreed because Dev was his friend. But he wanted Raj to know that being greedy is not very nice.

"Your fields will **produce** enough crops so that you will never be hungry. But they will not grow enough to make you rich," said Snake.

After that, Raj always shared his food with hungry people in the village.

Name: _____ Date: _____

Use "Snake's Lesson" to answer Numbers 1 through 8.

1 In the story, what does Snake think about Dev after he brings the milk?

Ⓐ He thinks Dev is generous.

Ⓑ He thinks Dev is rich enough.

Ⓒ He thinks Dev should work harder.

2 Read this sentence from the story.

> **The next day, when Dev woke up he witnessed something magnificent!**

Which word from the story has about the SAME meaning as *magnificent*?

Ⓐ amazing

Ⓑ full

Ⓒ healthy

3 What clue in the text helps you know that Dev is thankful for Snake's help?

Ⓐ He is happy that his crops grow.

Ⓑ He does what Snake tells him.

Ⓒ He brings Snake more milk.

GO ON →

Name: _____ Date: _____

4 What does Dev's friend, Raj, think when he sees Dev give milk to Snake?

Ⓐ Dev's crops will stop growing.

Ⓑ He can improve his own crops.

Ⓒ Snake is using milk to grow crops.

5 How do you know what Snake thinks of Raj's plans?

Ⓐ He refuses to help Raj.

Ⓑ He asks why Raj is giving him milk.

Ⓒ He says that Raj's crops are growing fine.

6 Read these sentences from the story.

> **Snake was horrified to hear this. He was very upset that Raj was so greedy.**

Which words from the sentences help you figure out what *horrified* means?

Ⓐ to hear this

Ⓑ was very upset

Ⓒ was so greedy

GO ON ➔

Exit Assessment • Unit 5

Grade 3   217

Name: _____ **Date:** _____

7 Read this paragraph from the story.

> "Your fields will produce enough crops so that you will never be hungry. But they will not grow enough to make you rich," said Snake.

Which clue words from the paragraph help you figure out what *produce* means?

Ⓐ never be hungry

Ⓑ grow enough

Ⓒ make you rich

8 What clue in the text helps you know that Raj learns to not be greedy?

Ⓐ He gives food to others.

Ⓑ He no longer asks Snake for help.

Ⓒ He does not have as much food as before.

Read "Jonas Salk" before you answer Numbers 9 through 15.

Jonas Salk

In the early 1900s, doctors in the United States faced a big problem. A disease was hurting hundreds of thousands of people. Many of those people were children. The disease was called polio.

Polio was easy to catch. It could keep children from learning to walk. Even President Franklin D. Roosevelt had polio. Everyone hoped someone would find a cure.

Many doctors studied the disease. One of these doctors was Jonas Salk. Salk first worked as part of a team that studied the flu. These doctors knew it was hard to cure diseases like the flu. But there was another solution!

Salk and others wanted to create a medicine that would stop people from getting the flu. This was called a vaccine. Salk thought about how important flu **prevention** was. He wanted to help stop people from getting polio, too.

In 1947, Salk began studying polio. He worked with other doctors and scientists. It was very important work. It took many years, but Salk did not get **discouraged**. He believed he could help fight polio. So he tried harder. Soon, Salk thought he had a vaccine that worked.

The first step was to test the vaccine. Most of the children who took the vaccine did not get polio! As a result, Salk knew it was time to tell people about it. Other doctors and scientists looked at his vaccine. They wanted to be sure the vaccine was safe.

In 1955, people in the United States began to get the vaccine. It was a big success! In just a few years, the number of people with polio was greatly reduced. Salk would not take any money for it. He wanted children all over to be safe from polio. Salk did not cure polio, but he did save many lives with his vaccine.

Other doctors looked at what Salk had done. Some of them found new ways to prevent polio, but Salk was the first person to give it away for free. Salk truly was a great American citizen!

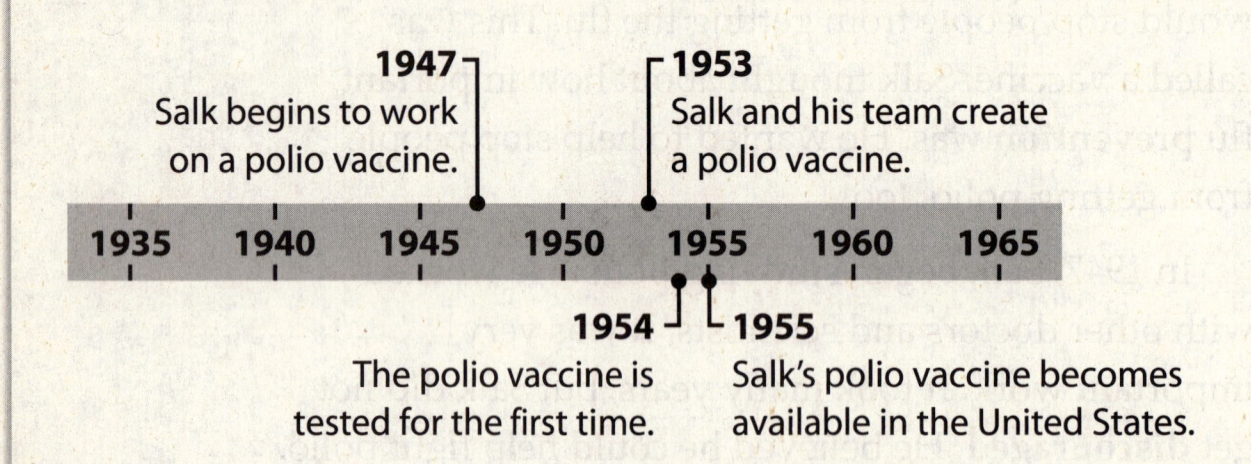

1947
Salk begins to work on a polio vaccine.

1953
Salk and his team create a polio vaccine.

1935 | 1940 | 1945 | 1950 | 1955 | 1960 | 1965

1954
The polio vaccine is tested for the first time.

1955
Salk's polio vaccine becomes available in the United States.

Name: _____   Date: _____

Use "Jonas Salk" to answer Numbers 9 through 15.

9 Which sentence from the article tells what the author thinks about polio?

　Ⓐ In the early 1900s, doctors in the United States faced a big problem.

　Ⓑ A disease was hurting hundreds of thousands of people.

　Ⓒ The disease was called polio.

10 Read this sentence from the article.

Salk thought about how important flu prevention was.

Which clue words from the article help you figure out what *prevention* means?

　Ⓐ it was hard to cure diseases

　Ⓑ others wanted to create a medicine

　Ⓒ stop people from getting the flu

11 Why did Salk begin studying polio?

　Ⓐ He felt discouraged after studying the flu.

　Ⓑ He wanted to earn a lot of money inventing a new vaccine.

　Ⓒ He believed he could find a cure for polio.

GO ON →

Exit Assessment • Unit 5   Grade 3   **221**

Name: _____ Date: _____

12 Which clue words from the text help you figure out what *discouraged* means?

Ⓐ other doctors and scientists

Ⓑ it took many years

Ⓒ believed he could help

13 According to the article, why did Salk try harder to create a polio vaccine?

Ⓐ He wanted to be the first to invent a vaccine.

Ⓑ He did not want to let people down.

Ⓒ He believed he could fight polio.

14 Why does the author think Salk was a great American citizen?

Ⓐ Salk gave away the polio vaccine for free.

Ⓑ There is now a cure for polio today.

Ⓒ Other people used Salk's work.

15 Which event happened first in the time line?

Ⓐ The polio vaccine was created.

Ⓑ The polio vaccine was tested for the first time.

Ⓒ The polio vaccine became available in the United States.

Read "Beth Grows Up in the Jazz Age" before you answer Numbers 1 through 7.

Beth Grows Up in the Jazz Age

"Please don't touch that radio!" I shouted nervously. I had caught my little sister reaching for the radio dial. "It's not a toy," I said.

I didn't want Cindy around when I listened to the radio. It was the most valuable thing in the world to me. That radio was my **treasure**.

It was the 1920s, an exciting time in the world. New inventions were one reason it was so exciting. My family got our first car and our first telephone.

Adults also had more free time than they had ever had before. So people wanted to have fun!

Some popular songs on the radio were **ridiculous**. One funny tune was about not having any bananas. Mom told me it was just nonsense, but she and Dad loved to sing along whenever it played.

The radio **communicated** all sorts of information about the world. My family listened to the news together. Dad and Cindy listened to baseball games. Reporters told me about the lives of glamorous and rich movie stars.

Name: _____   Date: _____

For me, the most exciting thing about the time was jazz music. Jazz singers sang beautiful songs that were not silly at all, and jazz bands played music that was fun to dance to. I practiced the newest dance steps to the radio every day.

But today, Cindy was being a bother. "It's no fair," she said. "Why can't I listen to the radio, too, Beth?"

She looked disappointed, so I let her be my dance partner.

I thought she would quickly become bored and leave me alone. But she concentrated hard and learned a few steps. I was proud of her, and we actually had fun.

When the song ended, we heard clapping. Mom was smiling in the doorway, and we all began to laugh.

I was surprised Cindy enjoyed dancing. I was also surprised how much fun it was teaching her something I loved. From that day on, I had a new dance partner.

Use "Beth Grows Up in the Jazz Age" to answer Numbers 1 through 7.

1 What does Beth think about the family radio at the beginning of the story?

Ⓐ She tries to keep it safe.

Ⓑ She thinks it is a toy.

Ⓒ She ignores it.

GO ON ➡

Name: _____ Date: _____

2 Read these sentences from the story.

> **It was the most valuable thing in the world to me. That radio was my treasure.**

Which clue word in the sentences helps you understand what *treasure* means?

Ⓐ valuable

Ⓑ thing

Ⓒ world

3 Which sentence from the story shows what Beth thinks about the 1920s?

Ⓐ I didn't want Cindy around when I listened to the radio.

Ⓑ New inventions were one reason it was so exciting.

Ⓒ One funny tune was about not having any bananas.

4 Which clue word in the story helps you understand the meaning of *ridiculous*?

Ⓐ free

Ⓑ nonsense

Ⓒ glamorous

Exit Assessment • Unit 6

GO ON →

Grade 3 225

Name: _____ Date: _____

5 Read this sentence from the story.

The radio communicated all sorts of information about the world.

Which word in the story means almost the SAME as *communicated*?

Ⓐ told

Ⓑ loved

Ⓒ listened

6 Which details describe what was MOST exciting for Beth?

Ⓐ Her family got new inventions like a car and a telephone.

Ⓑ Reporters on the radio described the lives of movie stars.

Ⓒ Jazz singers sang beautiful songs and bands played dance music.

7 What is the lesson of this story?

Ⓐ Jazz music is the best kind of music in the world.

Ⓑ Inventions make any time period interesting.

Ⓒ It is fun to share what you love with others.

GO ON →

Read "Alan Shepard" before you answer Numbers 8 through 15.

Alan Shepard

Alan Shepard grew up in New Hampshire. As a boy, he was interested in airplanes. He would bike ten miles from his home to an airport. There he did small jobs. His payments were rides in airplanes!

Shepard would become a **test pilot** in the Navy. A test pilot is someone who flies new types of planes to make sure they fly well. But Shepard had another goal. He wanted to fly to space. In 1959, he was picked by NASA to train to be an astronaut.

Shepard did well in training. He was the first to be picked for a space mission. The mission was called Freedom 7. On May 15, 1961, he took off in his spacecraft and made history. The flight took only 15 minutes. But Shepard became the first American in space.

Shepard was honored and **respected** for his historic flight. He was awarded a medal from the President. He also became famous, and parades were given in his honor.

Due to a medical problem, Shepard was not allowed on missions for nearly ten years. But he did not give up. Shepard had surgery to correct the problem. Then in 1971, he joined the Apollo 14 mission.

Unlike his first mission to space, Shepard did not fly alone. There were other astronauts on his team. They traveled further than Shepard's first mission. The Apollo 14 mission went to the Moon. This mission also took much longer than 15 minutes. The astronauts spent more than 33 hours on the Moon's surface alone.

Like his first mission, Shepard was celebrated for Apollo 14. He became the fifth person to walk on the Moon. He managed to have some fun, too. Americans were **astonished** and surprised when he became the first person to play golf on the Moon! He packed special golf clubs to do this.

Alan Shepard retired from NASA in 1974. President Bill Clinton called Alan Shepard, "one of the great heroes of modern America."

Name: _____ Date: _____

Use "Alan Shepard" to answer Numbers 8 through 15.

8 Which text evidence gives the definition of the keyword *test pilot*?

Ⓐ interested in airplanes

Ⓑ someone who flies new types of planes

Ⓒ picked by NASA to train to be an astronaut

9 Read this paragraph from the article.

> Shepard was honored and respected for his historic flight. He was awarded a medal from the President. He also became famous, and parades were given in his honor.

Which clue word in the paragraph means almost the SAME as *respected*?

Ⓐ honored

Ⓑ awarded

Ⓒ became

10 What problem did Alan Shepard face as an astronaut?

Ⓐ He wanted to be able to play golf on the Moon.

Ⓑ He was not allowed on a mission for nearly ten years.

Ⓒ He had to bike ten miles to an airport to do small jobs.

GO ON →

Exit Assessment · Unit 6   Grade 3   **229**

Name: _____ Date: _____

11 How was Shepard able to join the Apollo 14 mission?

Ⓐ He did very well in training.

Ⓑ He flew on many other space missions.

Ⓒ He had surgery to correct his medical problem.

12 How was the Apollo 14 mission DIFFERENT from Shepard's first mission?

Ⓐ On his first mission, Shepard flew alone.

Ⓑ On his first mission, Shepard flew to the Moon.

Ⓒ On his first mission, Shepard flew a spacecraft into space.

13 According to the article, how were both missions ALIKE for Shepard?

Ⓐ He traveled the same distance.

Ⓑ He was celebrated after both missions.

Ⓒ He walked in space during each mission.

GO ON →

Name: _____ Date: _____

14 How was Alan Shepard DIFFERENT from other astronauts at the time?

Ⓐ He saw the Moon.

Ⓑ He traveled into space.

Ⓒ He had fun and was silly.

15 Read these sentences from the article.

> **Americans were astonished and surprised when he became the first person to play golf on the Moon! He packed special golf clubs to do this.**

Which word from the sentences helps you understand the meaning of *astonished*?

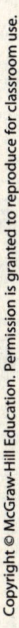

Ⓐ surprised

Ⓑ first

Ⓒ special

Fluency Assessment

Team Tryouts

Harry woke up. He rolled over and groaned. Getting up early was the worst part of training. The tryouts were only a day away. Harry had started last week. He'd been jogging every morning. His mom was a strong runner. Harry wanted to be one, too.

After school, Harry met his dad at the basketball courts. Harry's dad was a great basketball player. Harry was training for the basketball team, too. Harry and his dad played. Harry made a tough shot.

It was the night before the tryouts. Harry went to bed early. He stared at his uniform. He wondered if he could ever be a track star. Maybe he could become a basketball star, too!

- ✓ Why is Harry training?
- ✓ How is Harry's work connected to his parents?

Oral Reading Fluency Grade 3

Name: _____ Date: _____

Team Tryouts

9	Harry woke up. He rolled over and groaned. Getting
19	up early was the worst part of training. The tryouts
29	were only a day away. Harry had started last week.
38	He'd been jogging every morning. His mom was a
46	strong runner. Harry wanted to be one, too.
55	After school, Harry met his dad at the basketball
67	courts. Harry's dad was a great basketball player.
76	Harry was training for the basketball team, too. Harry
85	and his dad played. Harry made a tough shot.
95	It was the night before the tryouts. Harry went to
106	bed early. He stared at his uniform. He wondered if he
117	could ever be a track star. Maybe he could become a
120	basketball star, too!

✓ Why is Harry training?
✓ How is Harry's work connected to his parents?

Words Read	−	Errors	=	WCPM

☐ Fall (71 WCPM)
☐ Winter (92 WCPM)
☐ Spring (107 WCPM)

PROSODY

	L1	L2	L3	L4
Reading in Phrases	O	O	O	O
Pace	O	O	O	O
Syntax	O	O	O	O
Self-correction	O	O	O	O
Intonation	O	O	O	O

WCPM	÷	Words Read	=	Accuracy %

Oral Reading Fluency Assessment

Shipwrecks

Some people look for shipwrecks. Shipwrecks are ships that have sunk. These ships sank long ago. People look for treasures and objects from the past. They can find amazing things!

Some shipwrecks are easy to find. The ship sank in shallow water. It can be seen from the water's surface. Divers reach it easily.

But some ships sink in very deep water. They are hard to find. People spend a lot of time looking for them. They have to search vast areas of water.

First, searchers scan the water. They use special tools. They find where the ships sank. Then, divers go into the ocean. They take a closer look.

Submarines also help with the search. Searchers use cameras, videos, and radios. They record what they see.

- Which shipwrecks are most difficult to find?
- Why do people look for shipwrecks?

Oral Reading Fluency Grade 3

Name: _____ Date: _____

Shipwrecks

7	Some people look for shipwrecks. Shipwrecks are
16	ships that have sunk. These ships sank long ago.
25	People look for treasures and objects from the past.
30	They can find amazing things!
40	Some shipwrecks are easy to find. The ship sank in
50	shallow water. It can be seen from the water's surface.
54	Divers reach it easily.
64	But some ships sink in very deep water. They are
75	hard to find. People spend a lot of time looking for
84	them. They have to search vast areas of water.
93	First, searchers scan the water. They use special tools.
103	They find where the ships sank. Then, divers go into
110	the ocean. They take a closer look.
117	Submarines also help with the search. Searchers
125	use cameras, videos, and radios. They record what
127	they see.

✓ Which shipwrecks are most difficult to find?
✓ Why do people look for shipwrecks?

Words Read	-	Errors	=	WCPM

☐ Fall (71 WCPM)
☐ Winter (92 WCPM)
☐ Spring (107 WCPM)

PROSODY

	L1	L2	L3	L4
Reading in Phrases	O	O	O	O
Pace	O	O	O	O
Syntax	O	O	O	O
Self-correction	O	O	O	O
Intonation	O	O	O	O

WCPM	÷	Words Read	=	Accuracy %

Oral Reading Fluency Assessment

Oral Reading Fluency Grade 3

The Animal Rescue Center

"Catch him!" Lindy shouted.

The monkey jumped on top of the boxes. It tried to balance. But it could not. Crash! The boxes fell to the ground. The monkey landed safely.

It was another day in the animal rescue center. Lindy's mom picked up the monkey.

"It's good that he's jumping around," said Lindy's mom. "This means that his broken leg is healing. Soon we'll be able to take him back to the wild."

The animal rescue center was in the African grasslands. It was an hour away from the nearest town. Lindy's mom was a doctor for animals. They needed care all day and night. Lindy and her mom lived next to the center. Lindy loved it. She couldn't imagine living anywhere more fun.

- Why is it a good sign that the monkey is jumping around?
- What job does Lindy's mom have?

Oral Reading Fluency Grade 3

Name: _____ Date: _____

The Animal Rescue Center

4	"Catch him!" Lindy shouted.
15	The monkey jumped on top of the boxes. It tried to
26	balance. But it could not. Crash! The boxes fell to the
31	ground. The monkey landed safely.
40	It was another day in the animal rescue center.
46	Lindy's mom picked up the monkey.
54	"It's good that he's jumping around," said Lindy's
64	mom. "This means that his broken leg is healing. Soon
74	we'll be able to take him back to the wild."
82	The animal rescue center was in the African
92	grasslands. It was an hour away from the nearest town.
101	Lindy's mom was a doctor for animals. They needed
112	care all day and night. Lindy and her mom lived next
121	to the center. Lindy loved it. She couldn't imagine
125	living anywhere more fun.

✓ Why is it a good sign that the monkey is jumping around?
✓ What job does Lindy's mom have?

Words Read	-	Errors	=	WCPM

☐ Fall (71 WCPM)
☐ Winter (92 WCPM)
☐ Spring (107 WCPM)

WCPM	÷	Words Read	=	Accuracy %

PROSODY

	L1	L2	L3	L4
Reading in Phrases	o	o	o	o
Pace	o	o	o	o
Syntax	o	o	o	o
Self-correction	o	o	o	o
Intonation	o	o	o	o

Oral Reading Fluency Assessment

The Telephone

Today we can talk to anyone in the world. We can use phones or computers. How did people send messages before these devices existed? People used the telegraph. They could send messages quickly; however, they could not talk to each other.

People wanted a way to talk to someone far away. Then Alexander Graham Bell invented the telephone. Bell taught deaf children. He knew a lot about how people speak. He knew how they hear. He used what he knew to invent a telephone.

Bell worked on his design for years. He made the first call in 1876. The call was to his helper, Thomas Watson. Watson was in the room next door. Watson heard Bell's voice. Bell said, "Mr. Watson, come here! I need you!"

- How did people send long-distance messages before the telephone was invented?
- Who received the first phone call?

Oral Reading Fluency Grade 3

Name: _____ Date: _____

The Telephone

11	Today we can talk to anyone in the world. We can
19	use phones or computers. How did people send
27	messages before these devices existed? People used the
34	telegraph. They could send messages quickly; however,
41	they could not talk to each other.
51	People wanted a way to talk to someone far away.
58	Then Alexander Graham Bell invented the telephone.
68	Bell taught deaf children. He knew a lot about how
78	people speak. He knew how they hear. He used what
84	he knew to invent a telephone.
94	Bell worked on his design for years. He made the
105	first call in 1876. The call was to his helper, Thomas
114	Watson. Watson was in the room next door. Watson
123	heard Bell's voice. Bell said, "Mr. Watson, come here!
126	I need you!"

✓ How did people send long-distance messages before the telephone was invented?

✓ Who received the first phone call?

Words Read	-	Errors	=	WCPM

☐ Fall (71 WCPM)
☐ Winter (92 WCPM)
☐ Spring (107 WCPM)

WCPM	÷	Words Read	=	Accuracy %

PROSODY

	L1	L2	L3	L4
Reading in Phrases	O	O	O	O
Pace	O	O	O	O
Syntax	O	O	O	O
Self-correction	O	O	O	O
Intonation	O	O	O	O

Oral Reading Fluency Assessment

Karl's Trip

Karl hugged his mom good–bye.

"Have fun!" she called.

The train moved out of the city. Karl was going to visit his grandmother in the mountains. The train climbed through a forest of fir trees. Heavy snowfall covered their branches.

Karl looked out his window. The snow in the city was dirty and melted quickly. It looked different in the mountains. It was clean and fresh.

Grandmother hugged Karl at the station. Back home, she looked concerned. She said, "You must be hungry." She had baked spicy biscuits and a sweet purple plum tart.

It tasted delicious after the long ride. "Thank you," Karl said. He could already tell this was going to be a good trip.

✓ Where is Karl going to at the beginning of the story?

✓ What makes Karl think his trip will be good?

Oral Reading Fluency Grade 3

Name: _____   Date: _____

Karl's Trip

6	Karl hugged his mom good-bye.
10	"Have fun!" she called.
21	The train moved out of the city. Karl was going to
29	visit his grandmother in the mountains. The train
38	climbed through a forest of fir trees. Heavy snowfall
41	covered their branches.
51	Karl looked out his window. The snow in the city
61	was dirty and melted quickly. It looked different in the
67	mountains. It was clean and fresh.
74	Grandmother hugged Karl at the station. Back
83	home, she looked concerned. She said, "You must be
94	hungry." She had baked spicy biscuits and a sweet
97	purple plum tart.
106	It tasted delicious after the long ride. "Thank you,"
118	Karl said. He could already tell this was going to be a
120	good trip.

✓ Where is Karl going to at the beginning of the story?

✓ What makes Karl think his trip will be good?

Words Read	-	Errors	=	WCPM

☐ Fall (71 WCPM)
☐ Winter (92 WCPM)
☐ Spring (107 WCPM)

WCPM	÷	Words Read	=	Accuracy %

PROSODY

	L1	L2	L3	L4
Reading in Phrases	O	O	O	O
Pace	O	O	O	O
Syntax	O	O	O	O
Self-correction	O	O	O	O
Intonation	O	O	O	O

Oral Reading Fluency Assessment

Cats in History

Cats have been around for thousands of years. Today, we think of cats as house pets. Long ago, people thought they had special powers. Artists painted pictures of cats. They made sculptures. We can see these paintings and sculptures in museums today.

Cats were important in ancient Egypt. They were honored animals. The Egyptians loved cats. They even had a god with the head of a cat. People who hurt cats were punished. Cats were thought of as treasures.

The ancient Romans also liked cats. They thought cats were a symbol. They stood for being free. Cats could go in temples. No other animals could. There are still many cats in Rome even now. They are protected.

- How has thinking about cats changed over time?
- What did cats symbolize to the ancient Romans?

Oral Reading Fluency Grade 3

Name: _____ Date: _____

Cats in History

8	Cats have been around for thousands of years.
19	Today, we think of cats as house pets. Long ago, people
26	thought they had special powers. Artists painted
35	pictures of cats. They made sculptures. We can see
42	these paintings and sculptures in museums today.
50	Cats were important in ancient Egypt. They were
58	honored animals. The Egyptians loved cats. They even
71	had a god with the head of a cat. People who hurt cats
79	were punished. Cats were thought of as treasures.
87	The ancient Romans also liked cats. They thought
97	cats were a symbol. They stood for being free. Cats
107	could go in temples. No other animals could. There are
117	still many cats in Rome even now. They are protected.

✓ How has thinking about cats changed over time?
✓ What did cats symbolize to the ancient Romans?

Words Read	-	Errors	=	WCPM

☐ **Fall (71 WCPM)**
☐ **Winter (92 WCPM)**
☐ **Spring (107 WCPM)**

WCPM	÷	Words Read	=	Accuracy %

PROSODY

	L1	L2	L3	L4
Reading in Phrases	O	O	O	O
Pace	O	O	O	O
Syntax	O	O	O	O
Self-correction	O	O	O	O
Intonation	O	O	O	O

Oral Reading Fluency Assessment

Oral Reading Fluency Grade 3

Marta and the Gray Wolf

Once there was a girl named Marta. She lived near a big forest. Every day, her mother told her to avoid the forest. She would say, "Do not go in there. If you do, the Gray Wolf might get you."

One day, Marta was walking in the grass. She saw some flowers growing at the edge of the woods. They were so pretty. She had to pick them. Deeper into the forest, she saw some more. She picked them, too. All the while, she sang a sweet song to herself.

Suddenly, up rose the Gray Wolf. He said, "Little girl, sing that song again!" Marta did as she was told. Soon the Gray Wolf fell fast asleep. Her lovely song had lulled the wolf.

Marta raced out of the forest. She promised she would listen to her mother. And she never went into the forest again.

✓ What is the moral of this story?

✓ How does Marta escape the Gray Wolf?

Name: _____   Date: _____

Marta and the Gray Wolf

11	Once there was a girl named Marta. She lived near a
22	big forest. Every day, her mother told her to avoid the
34	forest. She would say, "Do not go in there. If you do,
40	the Gray Wolf might get you."
50	One day, Marta was walking in the grass. She saw
60	some flowers growing at the edge of the woods. They
71	were so pretty. She had to pick them. Deeper into the
81	forest, she saw some more. She picked them, too. All
90	the while, she sang a sweet song to herself.
99	Suddenly, up rose the Gray Wolf. He said, "Little
110	girl, sing that song again!" Marta did as she was told.
120	Soon the Gray Wolf fell fast asleep. Her lovely song
124	had lulled the wolf.
133	Marta raced out of the forest. She promised she
143	would listen to her mother. And she never went into
146	the forest again.

✓ What is the moral of this story?
✓ How does Marta escape the Gray Wolf?

Words Read	-	Errors	=	WCPM

☐ Fall (71 WCPM)
☐ Winter (92 WCPM)
☐ Spring (107 WCPM)

WCPM	÷	Words Read	=	Accuracy %

PROSODY

	L1	L2	L3	L4
Reading in Phrases	O	O	O	O
Pace	O	O	O	O
Syntax	O	O	O	O
Self-correction	O	O	O	O
Intonation	O	O	O	O

Oral Reading Fluency Assessment   Grade 3

Colors All Around Us

Colors help us understand the world around us.

Sunflowers have bright faces. They look like tiny suns. Their centers are filled with seeds. Yellow petals are around the seeds.

The artist Vincent van Gogh painted sunflowers. He was inspired by their colors. He made more than ten paintings of them. His paintings are treasures; you can find them in museums all over the world.

We often say the ocean is blue. However, water is colorless. Still, a clean ocean can look blue on a sunny day. Sometimes the ocean seems to change colors. Watch it on a stormy day. It may look gray. It may look green.

The color red can mean many things. Red can mean danger. Some animals are red for a reason. They are warning you. Their color shouts, "Stay away!"

- ✓ Who is Vincent van Gogh?
- ✓ What does the color red on some animals mean?

Oral Reading Fluency Grade 3

Name: _____   Date: _____

Colors All Around Us

8	Colors help us understand the world around us.
16	Sunflowers have bright faces. They look like tiny
25	suns. Their centers are filled with seeds. Yellow petals
29	are around the seeds.
37	The artist Vincent van Gogh painted sunflowers. He
47	was inspired by their colors. He made more than ten
56	paintings of them. His paintings are treasures; you can
64	find them in museums all over the world.
74	We often say the ocean is blue. However, water is
85	colorless. Still, a clean ocean can look blue on a sunny
93	day. Sometimes the ocean seems to change colors.
105	Watch it on a stormy day. It may look gray. It may
107	look green.
117	The color red can mean many things. Red can mean
127	danger. Some animals are red for a reason. They are
134	warning you. Their color shouts, "Stay away!"

✓ Who is Vincent van Gogh?

✓ What does the color red on some animals mean?

Words Read	-	Errors	=	WCPM

☐ Fall (71 WCPM)
☐ Winter (92 WCPM)
☐ Spring (107 WCPM)

WCPM	÷	Words Read	=	Accuracy %

PROSODY

	L1	L2	L3	L4
Reading in Phrases	O	O	O	O
Pace	O	O	O	O
Syntax	O	O	O	O
Self-correction	O	O	O	O
Intonation	O	O	O	O

Oral Reading Fluency Assessment

Antarctica

Travel as far south as you can go. You will reach the South Pole. The South Pole is in Antarctica. Antarctica is a continent covered with ice and snow. It is the coldest place on Earth.

Strong winds blow across Antarctica. It does not rain. It does not even snow very much. A vast layer of ice covers the land. This layer is called an *ice cap*. It is more than a mile thick. The ice cap extends into the sea.

The temperature in Antarctica is very cold. It is well below zero degrees! Water freezes at this temperature. Ice and snow don't melt in Antarctica.

Very few animals live in Antarctica. But many animals live in the oceans around the ice cap. Whales, seals, and sharks live there for part of the year.

- ✔ Where is the South Pole located?
- ✔ What is the MAIN idea of this article?

Oral Reading Fluency Grade 3

Name: _____   Date: _____

Antarctica

12	Travel as far south as you can go. You will reach the
21	South Pole. The South Pole is in Antarctica. Antarctica
32	is a continent covered with ice and snow. It is the
36	coldest place on Earth.
44	Strong winds blow across Antarctica. It does not
56	rain. It does not even snow very much. A vast layer of
69	ice covers the land. This layer is called an *ice cap*. It is
81	more than a mile thick. The ice cap extends into the sea.
91	The temperature in Antarctica is very cold. It is well
99	below zero degrees! Water freezes at this temperature.
106	Ice and snow don't melt in Antarctica.
114	Very few animals live in Antarctica. But many
124	animals live in the oceans around the ice cap. Whales,
134	seals, and sharks live there for part of the year.

✓ Where is the South Pole located?
✓ What is the MAIN idea of this article?

Words Read	-	Errors	=	WCPM

☐ Fall (71 WCPM)
☐ Winter (92 WCPM)
☐ Spring (107 WCPM)

WCPM	÷	Words Read	=	Accuracy %

PROSODY

	L1	L2	L3	L4
Reading in Phrases	O	O	O	O
Pace	O	O	O	O
Syntax	O	O	O	O
Self-correction	O	O	O	O
Intonation	O	O	O	O

Oral Reading Fluency Assessment

Something Special

There was something that Edie wanted to buy. But she did not have the money. So she rushed around doing work. She hoped doing chores would help her get the money.

Edie cleaned the family's towels and hung them out to dry. Dad helped, but still he paid her a dollar. Edie washed her brother's car. Her dog Spot helped her. He could fetch the hose and the sponge for her. Her brother helped, too. When she could not reach the roof of the car, he picked her up. She got three dollars from him when she was done.

Then Edie babysat for her cousin, Ben. Her aunt was making jam. While it simmered on the stove, Edie helped make a sandwich for Ben. She made him laugh with a cute song.

At the end of the week, Edie had enough money. She had ten dollars. Edie couldn't wait to go to the bookstore!

✓ How does Edie's dog help her with a job?

✓ What is Edie MOST LIKELY going to buy?

Oral Reading Fluency Grade 3

Name: _____ Date: _____

Something Special

9	There was something that Edie wanted to buy. But
19	she did not have the money. So she rushed around
28	doing work. She hoped doing chores would help her
31	get the money.
40	Edie cleaned the family's towels and hung them out
52	to dry. Dad helped, but still he paid her a dollar. Edie
61	washed her brother's car. Her dog Spot helped her.
72	He could fetch the hose and the sponge for her. Her
82	brother helped, too. When she could not reach the roof
94	of the car, he picked her up. She got three dollars from
99	him when she was done.
108	Then Edie babysat for her cousin, Ben. Her aunt
118	was making jam. While it simmered on the stove, Edie
128	helped make a sandwich for Ben. She made him laugh
132	with a cute song.
142	At the end of the week, Edie had enough money.
152	She had ten dollars. Edie couldn't wait to go to
154	the bookstore!

- How does Edie's dog help her with a job?
- What is Edie MOST LIKELY going to buy?

Words Read	-	Errors	=	WCPM

☐ Fall (71 WCPM)
☐ Winter (92 WCPM)
☐ Spring (107 WCPM)

WCPM	÷	Words Read	=	Accuracy %

PROSODY

	L1	L2	L3	L4
Reading in Phrases	○	○	○	○
Pace	○	○	○	○
Syntax	○	○	○	○
Self-correction	○	○	○	○
Intonation	○	○	○	○

Oral Reading Fluency Assessment

An Interesting Career

What are illustrators? These are the men and women who create the art that goes with books. The art from a book can bring back memories. It can help a reader picture characters.

Art in books helps to tell the story. There are many books that would not be the same without the art. The story would not change. However, the books would feel "unfinished" in some way.

Being an illustrator may seem like fun. But it is a job. The work must be done with care. Illustrators have to learn how to draw well. They need to show different things. They must draw people and animals that seem real.

The same person can be a book's author and illustrator. But that is often not the case. Sometimes the author writes the story first. Then the illustrator comes in and creates the art.

👉 How does art help a book?

👉 What are the challenges in being an illustrator?

Oral Reading Fluency Grade 3

Name: _____ Date: _____

An Interesting Career

9	What are illustrators? These are the men and women
20	who create the art that goes with books. The art from
31	a book can bring back memories. It can help a reader
33	picture characters.
44	Art in books helps to tell the story. There are many
55	books that would not be the same without the art. The
63	story would not change. However, the books would
68	feel "unfinished" in some way.
80	Being an illustrator may seem like fun. But it is a job.
90	The work must be done with care. Illustrators have to
100	learn how to draw well. They need to show different
108	things. They must draw people and animals that
110	seem real.
119	The same person can be a book's author and
129	illustrator. But that is often not the case. Sometimes the
138	author writes the story first. Then the illustrator comes
143	in and creates the art.

- How does art help a book?
- What are the challenges in being an illustrator?

Words Read	−	Errors	=	WCPM

☐ Fall (71 WCPM)
☐ Winter (92 WCPM)
☐ Spring (107 WCPM)

WCPM	÷	Words Read	=	Accuracy %

PROSODY

	L1	L2	L3	L4
Reading in Phrases	O	O	O	O
Pace	O	O	O	O
Syntax	O	O	O	O
Self-correction	O	O	O	O
Intonation	O	O	O	O

Oral Reading Fluency Assessment

Oral Reading Fluency Grade 3

Pip the Penguin

Pip is an emperor penguin. He started life as an egg. His mother, Peggy, laid the egg just before she went away. It was a beautiful white egg. She was very proud of it.

All the females left together. They traveled across the ice. They had to find food. They walked toward the sea under a stormy sky.

Pip's father, Philip, watched as the females left. He balanced Peggy's egg on his feet to keep it warm. His feathers fluttered as the wind blew. All of the other fathers in the colony had an egg to look after, too. They knew it was a very important job.

The females returned soon after Pip hatched. His mother recognized them from his father's call. She brought a lot of food.

✓ Why does Pip's mother leave before he hatches?
✓ What job do the fathers have?

Oral Reading Fluency Grade 3

Name: _____ Date: _____

Pip the Penguin

11	Pip is an emperor penguin. He started life as an egg.
21	His mother, Peggy, laid the egg just before she went
32	away. It was a beautiful white egg. She was very proud
34	of it.
43	All the females left together. They traveled across the
54	ice. They had to find food. They walked toward the sea
58	under a stormy sky.
66	Pip's father, Philip, watched as the females left.
77	He balanced Peggy's egg on his feet to keep it warm.
88	His feathers fluttered as the wind blew. All of the other
99	fathers in the colony had an egg to look after, too.
107	They knew it was a very important job.
114	The females returned soon after Pip hatched.
122	His mother recognized them from his father's call.
128	She brought a lot of food.

✏️ Why does Pip's mother leave before he hatches?
✏️ What job do the fathers have?

Words Read	-	Errors	=	WCPM

☐ Fall (71 WCPM)
☐ Winter (92 WCPM)
☐ Spring (107 WCPM)

WCPM	÷	Words Read	=	Accuracy %

PROSODY

	L1	L2	L3	L4
Reading in Phrases	O	O	O	O
Pace	O	O	O	O
Syntax	O	O	O	O
Self-correction	O	O	O	O
Intonation	O	O	O	O

Oral Reading Fluency Assessment

Australia

Australia is one of the seven continents of the world. Of the seven, it is the driest. It has ten deserts.

All deserts are dry. They are hot during the day and cold at night. Still, many plants and animals live in the desert. People can live in the desert, too.

The red kangaroo lives in the Australian desert. A female can carry its young in a pouch on its stomach. A pouch is like a pocket. Animals that have this type of pouch are called *marsupials*. There are more than 200 kinds of these animals living in or near Australia. One example is the numbat. But it is different from the red kangaroo. How? It does not have a pouch.

- How are the red kangaroo and numbat different?
- What is the driest continent?

Oral Reading Fluency Grade 3

Name: _____ Date: _____

Australia

10	Australia is one of the seven continents of the world.
21	Of the seven, it is the driest. It has ten deserts.
32	All deserts are dry. They are hot during the day and
43	cold at night. Still, many plants and animals live in the
51	desert. People can live in the desert, too.
59	The red kangaroo lives in the Australian desert.
71	A female can carry its young in a pouch on its stomach.
82	A pouch is like a pocket. Animals that have this type
91	of pouch are called *marsupials*. There are more than
101	200 kinds of these animals living in or near Australia.
112	One example is the numbat. But it is different from the
121	red kangaroo. How? It does not have a pouch.

✓ How are the red kangaroo and numbat different?
✓ What is the driest continent?

Words Read	-	Errors	=	WCPM

☐ Fall (71 WCPM)
☐ Winter (92 WCPM)
☐ Spring (107 WCPM)

PROSODY

	L1	L2	L3	L4
Reading in Phrases	O	O	O	O
Pace	O	O	O	O
Syntax	O	O	O	O
Self-correction	O	O	O	O
Intonation	O	O	O	O

WCPM	÷	Words Read	=	Accuracy %

Oral Reading Fluency Assessment

Liza's Ankle

A big storm left puddles everywhere. After school at soccer practice, Liza slipped in the mud. Ouch! Her ankle hurt. She couldn't get up. Coach Grimes put an ice pack on her ankle.

Liza's dad came. He drove her to the emergency room. "I hope you didn't break your ankle, honey," he said.

Liza felt like crying. She didn't want to miss the rest of the soccer season.

The doctor said Liza's ankle was sprained. It was not broken. He told Liza to stay off the soccer field for a few weeks until her ankle healed.

After a few weeks, Liza could play again. In her first game back, Liza scored the winning goal for her team.

"I feel as good as new. No, better than new!" she told her dad.

✔ What causes Liza's injury?

✔ What is most upsetting to Liza?

Oral Reading Fluency Grade 3

Name: _____ Date: _____

Liza's Ankle

8	A big storm left puddles everywhere. After school
18	at soccer practice, Liza slipped in the mud. Ouch! Her
28	ankle hurt. She couldn't get up. Coach Grimes put an
33	ice pack on her ankle.
42	Liza's dad came. He drove her to the emergency
51	room. "I hope you didn't break your ankle, honey,"
53	he said.
64	Liza felt like crying. She didn't want to miss the rest
68	of the soccer season.
78	The doctor said Liza's ankle was sprained. It was not
90	broken. He told Liza to stay off the soccer field for a
96	few weeks until her ankle healed.
107	After a few weeks, Liza could play again. In her first
117	game back, Liza scored the winning goal for her team.
129	"I feel as good as new. No, better than new!" she told
131	her dad.

✓ What causes Liza's injury?
✓ What is most upsetting to Liza?

Words Read	−	Errors	=	WCPM

☐ Fall (71 WCPM)
☐ Winter (92 WCPM)
☐ Spring (107 WCPM)

WCPM	÷	Words Read	=	Accuracy %

PROSODY

	L1	L2	L3	L4
Reading in Phrases	O	O	O	O
Pace	O	O	O	O
Syntax	O	O	O	O
Self-correction	O	O	O	O
Intonation	O	O	O	O

Oral Reading Fluency Assessment

Hummingbirds

Hummingbirds do not actually hum. But they do beat their wings very fast. This makes a humming sound. If you see a hummingbird, stop and listen. You will hear a buzzing sound. That is the sound of the hummingbird's wings!

Hummingbirds are tiny. They are about the size of large bumblebees. Hummingbirds build small nests. They build the nests with moss, tree bark, leaves and feathers. The nests are very small. Most people don't even notice them because they are so small. The inside of the nest is soft. The mother hummingbird lays two eggs. Soon the baby hummingbirds hatch. When they hatch, the mother hummingbird needs to care for them. The father hummingbird does not share the work.

Hummingbirds have long bills to drink nectar from flowers. Nectar is a sweet juice. They must drink a lot of nectar. They need it to fly. It gives them energy.

- ✓ Why are hummingbird nests difficult to notice?
- ✓ Why do hummingbirds have long bills?

Oral Reading Fluency Grade 3

Name: _____ Date: _____

Hummingbirds

8	Hummingbirds do not actually hum. But they do
17	beat their wings very fast. This makes a humming
26	sound. If you see a hummingbird, stop and listen.
38	You will hear a buzzing sound. That is the sound of the
40	hummingbird's wings!
49	Hummingbirds are tiny. They are about the size of
55	large bumblebees. Hummingbirds build small nests.
65	They build the nests with moss, tree bark, leaves and
74	feathers. The nests are very small. Most people don't
84	even notice them because they are so small. The inside
94	of the nest is soft. The mother hummingbird lays two
102	eggs. Soon the baby hummingbirds hatch. When they
111	hatch, the mother hummingbird needs to care for them.
119	The father hummingbird does not share the work.
127	Hummingbirds have long bills to drink nectar from
138	flowers. Nectar is a sweet juice. They must drink a lot
149	of nectar. They need it to fly. It gives them energy.

✓ Why are hummingbird nests difficult to notice?
✓ Why do hummingbirds have long bills?

Words Read	−	Errors	=	WCPM

☐ Fall (71 WCPM)
☐ Winter (92 WCPM)
☐ Spring (107 WCPM)

WCPM	÷	Words Read	=	Accuracy %

PROSODY

	L1	L2	L3	L4
Reading in Phrases	○	○	○	○
Pace	○	○	○	○
Syntax	○	○	○	○
Self-correction	○	○	○	○
Intonation	○	○	○	○

Oral Reading Fluency Assessment

Mouse, Rat, and Owl

Mouse and Rat were playing outside. Then they heard someone shout, "Go away! You are too loud." They looked all around, but they could not see who was talking. Then the voice said, "Look up here in the tree."

Mouse and Rat looked up and saw a brown owl. Owl said, "You are making too much noise. I am trying to sleep now."

"But it's light out," said Mouse.

"Yes, I know. Owls sleep in the day. We hunt at night," said Owl.

Mouse and Rat were surprised. They thought everyone slept at night.

Owl startled them out of their thoughts. "Now go away!" he shouted. "And be quiet down there, or I will hunt for you tonight!" Mouse and Rat ran away so that Owl would not be able to find them later.

- 👉 Why is Owl upset?
- 👉 What surprises Mouse and Rat?

Oral Reading Fluency Grade 3

Name: _____ Date: _____

Mouse, Rat, and Owl

8	Mouse and Rat were playing outside. Then they
17	heard someone shout, "Go away! You are too loud."
27	They looked all around, but they could not see who
37	was talking. Then the voice said, "Look up here in
39	the tree."
50	Mouse and Rat looked up and saw a brown owl. Owl
61	said, "You are making too much noise. I am trying to
63	sleep now."
69	"But it's light out," said Mouse.
80	"Yes, I know. Owls sleep in the day. We hunt at
83	night," said Owl.
90	Mouse and Rat were surprised. They thought
94	everyone slept at night.
103	Owl startled them out of their thoughts. "Now go
114	away!" he shouted. "And be quiet down there, or I will
125	hunt for you tonight!" Mouse and Rat ran away so that
134	Owl would not be able to find them later.

✓ Why is Owl upset?
✓ What surprises Mouse and Rat?

Words Read	-	Errors	=	WCPM

☐ Fall (71 WCPM)
☐ Winter (92 WCPM)
☐ Spring (107 WCPM)

WCPM	÷	Words Read	=	Accuracy %

PROSODY

	L1	L2	L3	L4
Reading in Phrases	O	O	O	O
Pace	O	O	O	O
Syntax	O	O	O	O
Self-correction	O	O	O	O
Intonation	O	O	O	O

Oral Reading Fluency Assessment

Lin's Painting

"You're doing very well, class," said Ms. Tallant.

The second graders were working on a mural. It was a picture of their town, Greenville.

Each group was painting a panel. Each panel was put up on the wall as it was finished. Their town had spread across the walls of their classroom!

Lin was working hard on her part of the panel. She carefully painted the park, her favorite part of town. She put herself in the picture with her dog, Gus.

The bell rang. Everyone except Lin packed up for recess.

"It is recess time, Lin," said Ms. Tallant. "You need to get some fresh air."

"Yes, Ms. Tallant," Lin sighed. She put down her paint brush, put away her paints, and put on her coat. She didn't really want to play outside with her classmates. She would rather play in her own park with Gus.

✓ What is Ms. Tallant's class creating?

✓ Why is Lin not excited about recess?

Oral Reading Fluency Grade 3

Name: _____ Date: _____

Lin's Painting

8	"You're doing very well, class," said Ms. Tallant.
18	The second graders were working on a mural. It was
24	a picture of their town, Greenville.
33	Each group was painting a panel. Each panel was
45	put up on the wall as it was finished. Their town had
52	spread across the walls of their classroom!
63	Lin was working hard on her part of the panel. She
72	carefully painted the park, her favorite part of town.
82	She put herself in the picture with her dog, Gus.
90	The bell rang. Everyone except Lin packed up
92	for recess.
102	"It is recess time, Lin," said Ms. Tallant. "You need
107	to get some fresh air."
116	"Yes, Ms. Tallant," Lin sighed. She put down her
126	paint brush, put away her paints, and put on her
135	coat. She didn't really want to play outside with
144	her classmates. She would rather play in her own
147	park with Gus.

✓ What is Ms. Tallant's class creating?
✓ Why is Lin not excited about recess?

Words Read	−	Errors	=	WCPM

☐ Fall (71 WCPM)
☐ Winter (92 WCPM)
☐ Spring (107 WCPM)

WCPM	÷	Words Read	=	Accuracy %

PROSODY

	L1	L2	L3	L4
Reading in Phrases	O	O	O	O
Pace	O	O	O	O
Syntax	O	O	O	O
Self-correction	O	O	O	O
Intonation	O	O	O	O

Oral Reading Fluency Assessment

The Talking Glove

People who cannot hear have other ways of talking. For instance, many deaf people sign with their hands. But some people do not understand signing. How can deaf people who sign talk with these people?

Scientists are working on solutions. For example, a scientist invented a special glove. A computer in the glove translates sign language. Here's how it works. First, a person puts on the glove. This person signs with his or her hands. Then the glove translates the hand motions into words. It displays these words on a screen. It reads the words through a speaker, too. People nearby may not understand signing. But they can read and hear what the glove says.

Right now this special glove only works in English. But soon it will work in other languages. Deaf and hearing people from many cultures will be able to "talk" to each other.

✓ How is the talking glove a solution to a problem?

✓ How does the talking glove work?

Oral Reading Fluency Grade 3

Name: _____ Date: _____

The Talking Glove

9	People who cannot hear have other ways of talking.
18	For instance, many deaf people sign with their hands.
27	But some people do not understand signing. How can
35	deaf people who sign talk with these people?
43	Scientists are working on solutions. For example, a
52	scientist invented a special glove. A computer in the
60	glove translates sign language. Here's how it works.
70	First, a person puts on the glove. This person signs
80	with his or her hands. Then the glove translates the
89	hand motions into words. It displays these words on
99	a screen. It reads the words through a speaker, too.
107	People nearby may not understand signing. But they
115	can read and hear what the glove says.
124	Right now this special glove only works in English.
134	But soon it will work in other languages. Deaf and
143	hearing people from many cultures will be able to
147	"talk" to each other.

✓ How is the talking glove a solution to a problem?
✓ How does the talking glove work?

Words Read	−	Errors	=	WCPM

☐ Fall (71 WCPM)
☐ Winter (92 WCPM)
☐ Spring (107 WCPM)

WCPM	÷	Words Read	=	Accuracy %

PROSODY

	L1	L2	L3	L4
Reading in Phrases	○	○	○	○
Pace	○	○	○	○
Syntax	○	○	○	○
Self-correction	○	○	○	○
Intonation	○	○	○	○

Oral Reading Fluency Assessment

The Dirty Creek

"This creek is really dirty," said Marcella.

Mark frowned. "Look at how the reeds are thinning," he said. "I bet that's because the litter is getting in the way of the plants. If this doesn't get cleaned up, all the plants will die. The animals living here will lose their home."

"Yes," said Marcella. "Someone should clean it up."

"Then what are we waiting for?" asked Mark.

Marcella and Mark borrowed a garden rake, large plastic bags, and a box of plastic gloves from their mother. Then they began to clear the litter from the creek bed. Next, they scooped up bottles and cans from the water. Then they picked up garbage from among the reeds. They were so busy that at first they didn't notice they were being watched. Marcella looked up.

"We have company," she said to Mark.

They both smiled as their mom walked over to them, ready to help.

- Why are Mark and Marcella concerned?
- What do Mark and Marcella decide to do?

Oral Reading Fluency Grade 3

Name: _____ Date: _____

The Dirty Creek

7	"This creek is really dirty," said Marcella.
16	Mark frowned. "Look at how the reeds are thinning,"
28	he said. "I bet that's because the litter is getting in the
39	way of the plants. If this doesn't get cleaned up, all
49	the plants will die. The animals living here will lose
51	their home."
59	"Yes," said Marcella. "Someone should clean it up."
67	"Then what are we waiting for?" asked Mark.
75	Marcella and Mark borrowed a garden rake, large
85	plastic bags, and a box of plastic gloves from their
95	mother. Then they began to clear the litter from the
105	creek bed. Next, they scooped up bottles and cans from
114	the water. Then they picked up garbage from among
125	the reeds. They were so busy that at first they didn't
133	notice they were being watched. Marcella looked up.
140	"We have company," she said to Mark.
150	They both smiled as their mom walked over to them,
153	ready to help.

- Why are Mark and Marcella concerned?
- What do Mark and Marcella decide to do?

Words Read	-	Errors	=	WCPM

☐ Fall (71 WCPM)
☐ Winter (92 WCPM)
☐ Spring (107 WCPM)

WCPM	÷	Words Read	=	Accuracy %

PROSODY

	L1	L2	L3	L4
Reading in Phrases	O	O	O	O
Pace	O	O	O	O
Syntax	O	O	O	O
Self-correction	O	O	O	O
Intonation	O	O	O	O

Oral Reading Fluency Assessment

Boat Safety

Boat rides are a great way to be on the water without getting wet. A boat ride can be a fast way to get to places. Many people like to fish from a boat. There are rules to follow so you can stay safe while boating.

First, never go on a boat without an adult. Always check the weather before you leave, and don't get in a boat if a storm is coming.

When you are in the boat, you must wear a life jacket. Be careful when you get in and out of a boat. It is easy to slip and fall. Don't jump in a boat. The boat can tip over. And ask an adult before jumping or diving from a boat. You need to watch out. Rocks or other sharp objects can be under the water.

What do you do if there is an issue when you are out at sea? Reach the U.S. Coast Guard. The Coast Guard watches over the coastline and seas of America.

✓ What must you always wear on a boat?

✓ Why can diving from a boat be risky?

Boat Safety

12	Boat rides are a great way to be on the water without
25	getting wet. A boat ride can be a fast way to get to
36	places. Many people like to fish from a boat. There are
46	rules to follow so you can stay safe while boating.
56	First, never go on a boat without an adult. Always
67	check the weather before you leave, and don't get in a
73	boat if a storm is coming.
84	When you are in the boat, you must wear a life
96	jacket. Be careful when you get in and out of a boat.
109	It is easy to slip and fall. Don't jump in a boat. The
120	boat can tip over. And ask an adult before jumping or
131	diving from a boat. You need to watch out. Rocks or
139	other sharp objects can be under the water.
152	What do you do if there is an issue when you are out
162	at sea? Reach the U.S. Coast Guard. The Coast Guard
170	watches over the coastline and seas of America.

- ✓ What must you always wear on a boat?
- ✓ Why can diving from a boat be risky?

Words Read	-	Errors	=	WCPM

☐ Fall (71 WCPM)
☐ Winter (92 WCPM)
☐ Spring (107 WCPM)

WCPM	÷	Words Read	=	Accuracy %

PROSODY

	L1	L2	L3	L4
Reading in Phrases	O	O	O	O
Pace	O	O	O	O
Syntax	O	O	O	O
Self-correction	O	O	O	O
Intonation	O	O	O	O

Oral Reading Fluency Assessment

Football Tryouts

Bindi and Amy were practicing for touch football tryouts, but Amy was having trouble throwing the ball straight.

"Come on, Amy," shouted Bindi. "Throw the football to me!"

Amy threw the football, but it dropped as soon as it left her hands and tumbled slowly along the ground. She walked away and sat down on a bench. Amy didn't like touch football tryouts. Everyone threw better than she did. Plus, Amy had stayed home sick from school the last two weeks. She still felt weak and not totally healthy.

Bindi ran over. "Come on, Amy," he said. "We're not going to be on the same team if you don't try harder."

Amy shook her head. "I just want to sit and watch right now," she explained.

"I know it's hard, Amy," said Bindi. "But if we work together, I know you'll get better. I promise! The team won't feel the same to me if you are not on it."

✓ What is Bindi's promise?

✓ What text evidence supports the idea that Bindi and Amy are friends?

Oral Reading Fluency Grade 3

Name: _____ Date: _____

Football Tryouts

8	Bindi and Amy were practicing for touch football
16	tryouts, but Amy was having trouble throwing the
18	ball straight.
26	"Come on, Amy," shouted Bindi. "Throw the football
28	to me!"
39	Amy threw the football, but it dropped as soon as it
48	left her hands and tumbled slowly along the ground.
58	She walked away and sat down on a bench. Amy
65	didn't like touch football tryouts. Everyone threw
75	better than she did. Plus, Amy had stayed home sick
86	from school the last two weeks. She still felt weak and
89	not totally healthy.
99	Bindi ran over. "Come on, Amy," he said. "We're not
111	going to be on the same team if you don't try harder."
122	Amy shook her head. "I just want to sit and watch
126	right now," she explained.
137	"I know it's hard, Amy," said Bindi. "But if we work
147	together, I know you'll get better. I promise! The team
159	won't feel the same to me if you are not on it."

✓ What is Bindi's promise?

✓ What text evidence supports the idea that Bindi and Amy are friends?

Words Read	−	Errors	=	WCPM

☐ Fall (71 WCPM)
☐ Winter (92 WCPM)
☐ Spring (107 WCPM)

WCPM	÷	Words Read	=	Accuracy %

PROSODY

	L1	L2	L3	L4
Reading in Phrases	O	O	O	O
Pace	O	O	O	O
Syntax	O	O	O	O
Self-correction	O	O	O	O
Intonation	O	O	O	O

Oral Reading Fluency Assessment

The Discovery of Troy

Around 3,000 years ago, Greece and Troy were at war. Troy was an ancient city. It lay on the coast of what is now Turkey.

According to legend, 10,000 Greek ships sailed to Troy. Greece and Troy fought for ten years. The war ended when some Greek soldiers came up with a plan. They built a huge wooden horse and hid inside. The people of Troy thought the horse was a gift. They pulled it inside the city walls. At night, the Greek soldiers climbed out. Then they attacked the city.

Years later, many people thought Troy was just a legend. But a German archaeologist changed their minds. In 1871, he went to the coast of Turkey. He began digging at a small hill. Inside the hill, he found the remains of nine ancient cities. One city had large stone walls. He thought he had found the walls of Troy.

- How did the Greek soldiers trick the people of Troy?
- Where was Troy located?

Oral Reading Fluency Grade 3

Name: _____ Date: _____

The Discovery of Troy

9	Around 3,000 years ago, Greece and Troy were at
21	war. Troy was an ancient city. It lay on the coast of
25	what is now Turkey.
33	According to legend, 10,000 Greek ships sailed to
43	Troy. Greece and Troy fought for ten years. The war
52	ended when some Greek soldiers came up with a
62	plan. They built a huge wooden horse and hid inside.
73	The people of Troy thought the horse was a gift. They
83	pulled it inside the city walls. At night, the Greek
91	soldiers climbed out. Then they attacked the city.
100	Years later, many people thought Troy was just a
107	legend. But a German archaeologist changed their
118	minds. In 1871, he went to the coast of Turkey. He
129	began digging at a small hill. Inside the hill, he found
139	the remains of nine ancient cities. One city had large
150	stone walls. He thought he had found the walls of Troy.

- ✓ How did the Greek soldiers trick the people of Troy?
- ✓ Where was Troy located?

Words Read	−	Errors	=	WCPM

☐ Fall (71 WCPM)
☐ Winter (92 WCPM)
☐ Spring (107 WCPM)

WCPM	÷	Words Read	=	Accuracy %

PROSODY

	L1	L2	L3	L4
Reading in Phrases	O	O	O	O
Pace	O	O	O	O
Syntax	O	O	O	O
Self-correction	O	O	O	O
Intonation	O	O	O	O

Oral Reading Fluency Assessment

Mrs. Bailey's Store

Mrs. Bailey's country store stood at the end of Cherry Blossom Lane. It was famous for its beautiful knitted goods. If you looked around the store, you were sure to see Mrs. Bailey. She was always knitting or cleaning.

One morning, Mrs. Bailey was dusting and fussing even more than usual. Her new helper was about to arrive.

Clip-clop-trip-trop went the sound of the hooves up the pebbled path.

"She's here!" Mrs. Bailey said excitedly. She hung up her duster and ran to the front door. She flung open the door and bounced down the path. She passed the vegetable garden and the flower garden. She passed the old oak tree that shaded the yard. Finally, she reached the front gate. It swung open with a creak.

"Welcome, Sarah," Mrs. Bailey called out eagerly. "Follow me inside, and let's get started!"

- Why is Mrs. Bailey cleaning up at the start of the story?
- Who is Sarah?

Oral Reading Fluency Grade 3

Name: _____ Date: _____

Mrs. Bailey's Store

10	Mrs. Bailey's country store stood at the end of Cherry
19	Blossom Lane. It was famous for its beautiful knitted
30	goods. If you looked around the store, you were sure to
39	see Mrs. Bailey. She was always knitting or cleaning.
47	One morning, Mrs. Bailey was dusting and fussing
56	even more than usual. Her new helper was about
58	to arrive.
69	*Clip-clop-trip-trop* went the sound of the hooves up
72	the pebbled path.
80	"She's here!" Mrs. Bailey said excitedly. She hung
92	up her duster and ran to the front door. She flung open
102	the door and bounced down the path. She passed the
110	vegetable garden and the flower garden. She passed
120	the old oak tree that shaded the yard. Finally, she
130	reached the front gate. It swung open with a creak.
137	"Welcome, Sarah," Mrs. Bailey called out eagerly.
144	"Follow me inside, and let's get started!"

✓ Why is Mrs. Bailey cleaning up at the start of the story?
✓ Who is Sarah?

Words Read	−	Errors	=	WCPM

☐ Fall (71 WCPM)
☐ Winter (92 WCPM)
☐ Spring (107 WCPM)

PROSODY

	L1	L2	L3	L4
Reading in Phrases	o	o	o	o
Pace	o	o	o	o
Syntax	o	o	o	o
Self-correction	o	o	o	o
Intonation	o	o	o	o

WCPM	÷	Words Read	=	Accuracy %

Oral Reading Fluency Assessment

Henry Ford's Assembly Line

In the 1880s, two German inventors built the first modern cars. These cars were a lot like cars today. But another important change came in 1913. This change affected how cars were made.

The first cars were very expensive. Many people could not buy them. Henry Ford changed that. Ford was an American car maker. He started making cars on an assembly line. On an assembly line, each worker only does one job. This is a much faster way of working. It is also much cheaper. Today, many cars are made this way in factories.

Before assembly lines, Ford's workers built a single car in 12 hours. After, it only took 90 minutes. By the 1920s, Ford made one car every 43 seconds! Ford cars were cheap to make. As a result, they were also cheap to buy. More people were able to own cars.

✔ What change did Ford bring to making cars?

✔ How did Ford's idea result in more people owning cars?

Oral Reading Fluency Grade 3

Name: _____ Date: _____

Henry Ford's Assembly Line

9	In the 1880s, two German inventors built the first
20	modern cars. These cars were a lot like cars today. But
28	another important change came in 1913. This change
33	affected how cars were made.
41	The first cars were very expensive. Many people
50	could not buy them. Henry Ford changed that. Ford
58	was an American car maker. He started making
68	cars on an assembly line. On an assembly line, each
80	worker only does one job. This is a much faster way of
90	working. It is also much cheaper. Today, many cars are
95	made this way in factories.
103	Before assembly lines, Ford's workers built a single
115	car in 12 hours. After, it only took 90 minutes. By the
125	1920s, Ford made one car every 43 seconds! Ford cars
136	were cheap to make. As a result, they were also cheap
145	to buy. More people were able to own cars.

✓ What change did Ford bring to making cars?
✓ How did Ford's idea result in more people owning cars?

Words Read	-	Errors	=	WCPM

☐ Fall (71 WCPM)
☐ Winter (92 WCPM)
☐ Spring (107 WCPM)

WCPM	÷	Words Read	=	Accuracy %

PROSODY

	L1	L2	L3	L4
Reading in Phrases	O	O	O	O
Pace	O	O	O	O
Syntax	O	O	O	O
Self-correction	O	O	O	O
Intonation	O	O	O	O

Oral Reading Fluency Assessment

Scoring Sheets and Answer Keys

Name: _____   Date: _____

WEEKLY ASSESSMENT SCORING SHEET   UNIT ___ WEEK ___

Item	Content Focus/CCSS	Score	Comments
1			
2			
3			
4			
5			

Name: _____   Date: _____

MID-UNIT ASSESSMENT SCORING SHEET   UNIT __

Item	Content Focus/CCSS	Score	Comments
1			
2			
3			
4			
5			
6			
7			
8			
9			
10			

Assessment · Scoring Sheet

Name: _____ Date: _____

UNIT ASSESSMENT SCORING SHEET   UNIT __

Item	Content Focus/CCSS	Score	Comments
1			
2			
3			
4			
5			
6			
7			
8			
9			
10			
11			
12			
13			
14			
15			

Name: _____   Date: _____

EXIT ASSESSMENT SCORING SHEET   **UNIT __**

Item	Content Focus/CCSS	Score	Comments
1			
2			
3			
4			
5			
6			
7			
8			
9			
10			
11			
12			
13			
14			
15			

Assessment • Scoring Sheet

Weekly Assessment Answer Key

UNIT 1 WEEK 1

Item #	Content Focus	CCSS
1	Vocabulary: Context Clues	L.3.4a
2	Character	RL.3.3
3	Vocabulary: Context Clues	L.3.4a
4	Character	RL.3.3
5	Character	RL.3.3

Suggested Responses:

1. **Text Evidence:** happy
2. **Text Evidence:** "I want a new place to call home," he said.
3. Tom is scared of heights.
   Text Evidence: found out
4. It is cool in summer.
5. He learns that he is always at home in his shell.

UNIT 1 WEEK 2

Item #	Content Focus	CCSS
1	Sequence	RL.3.3
2	Vocabulary: Context Clues	L.3.4a
3	Sequence	RL.3.3
4	Vocabulary: Context Clues	L.3.4a
5	Sequence	RL.3.3

Suggested Responses:

1. She does not have a gift for her brother.
   Text Evidence: "I do not have a gift," said Joy.
2. **Text Evidence:** having a good time
3. Joy gives her brother the bracelet she made.
   Text Evidence: Joy went over to her brother. She held a red paper bracelet. She put it on his wrist.
4. **Text Evidence:** important custom
5. Joy feels happy.
   Text Evidence: Joy smiled. She felt happy again.

UNIT 1 WEEK 3

Item #	Content Focus	CCSS
1	Vocabulary: Context Clues	L.3.4a
2	Sequence	RI.3.3
3	Sequence	RI.3.3
4	Vocabulary: Context Clues	L.3.4a
5	Sequence	RI.3.3

Suggested Responses:

1. **Text Evidence:** school
   someone you go to school with
2. Sofia has to do homework.
   Text Evidence: Next, I have a piano lesson.
3. Sofia has to help get ready for her sister's party.
   Text Evidence: Last
4. **Text Evidence:** I am helping set up the hall.
   give to or help with something
5. She will go to Kate's house.

UNIT 1 WEEK 4

Item #	Content Focus	CCSS
1	Cause and Effect	RI.3.3
2	Cause and Effect	RI.3.3
3	Vocabulary: Context Clues	L.3.4a
4	Cause and Effect	RI.3.3
5	Vocabulary: Context Clues	L.3.4a

Suggested Responses:

1. The babies stayed close to their mothers.
   Text Evidence: As a result
2. The baby slipped.
   Text Evidence: But the baby kept slipping.
3. **Text Evidence:** problem
   an answer
4. **Text Evidence:** They could keep their arms free for other things.
5. **Text Evidence:** easy

Weekly Assessment • Answer Key

UNIT 1 WEEK 5

Item #	Content Focus	CCSS
1	Vocabulary: Context Clues	L.3.4a
2	Main Idea and Key Details	RI.3.2
3	Vocabulary: Context Clues	L.3.4a
4	Main Idea and Key Details	RI.3.2
5	Main Idea and Key Details	RI.3.2

Suggested Responses:

1. **Text Evidence:** almost 400 feet tall
2. **Text Evidence:** William Kent wanted to help; He wanted to keep the forest safe for people to enjoy.
3. **Text Evidence:** national; keep the forest safe
   a place that is protected by the country or government
4. **Text Evidence:** January 9, 1908
   People go to see the redwoods.
5. The Muir Woods National Monument was created to help protect the redwoods.
   Text Evidence: People began to worry. They did not want to lose these trees.
   He bought a redwood forest in 1905. Then he gave the forest to the country.

UNIT 2 WEEK 1

Item #	Content Focus	CCSS
1	Theme	RL.3.2
2	Vocabulary: Context Clues	L.3.4a
3	Theme	RL.3.2
4	Vocabulary: Context Clues	L.3.4a
5	Theme	RL.3.2

Suggested Responses:

1. Cat's boat is too small for the big waves of the sea.
2. **Text Evidence:** try
3. The wind is strong and the waves are big.
   Text Evidence: Fish turned Cat's boat around. He pulled the boat back to the river where it was safe.
4. **Text Evidence:** shy
   after she goes out to sea
5. Listen to a friend who knows better than you.
   Text Evidence: Cat should have listened to her friend. Fish knew more about the sea than anyone.

UNIT 2 WEEK 2

Item #	Content Focus	CCSS
1	Vocabulary: Context Clues	L.3.4a
2	Theme	RL.3.2
3	Vocabulary: Context Clues	L.3.4a
4	Theme	RL.3.2
5	Theme	RL.3.2

Suggested Responses:

1. **Text Evidence:** came from other countries
2. He does not want to leave his friends.
   Text Evidence: "I will miss my friends," he said.
3. **Text Evidence:** left
   came to
4. **Text Evidence:** There were many new kids at the school.
5. Tom learns that you can find friends anywhere you go.
   Text Evidence:
   (paragraph 4) "You will make new friends," Dad said. "You can find friends anywhere you go."
   (paragraph 7) "You can find friends anywhere you go."

UNIT 2 WEEK 3

Item #	Content Focus	CCSS
1	Vocabulary: Context Clues	L.3.4a
2	Author's Point of View	RI.3.6
3	Author's Point of View	RI.3.6
4	Vocabulary: Context Clues	L.3.4a
5	Author's Point of View	RI.3.6

Suggested Responses:

1. **Text Evidence:** rules our country
2. **Text Evidence:** Each branch is important.
3. **Text Evidence:** Laws Signed by President
   The graph shows that the president has an important job of helping to create many new laws.
4. **Text Evidence:** chooses
5. None of the branches has more power than the others.
   Text Evidence: The branches have different powers. No branch has too much power.

Weekly Assessment • Answer Key   Grade 3   **291**

UNIT 2 WEEK 4

Item #	Content Focus	CCSS
1	Author's Point of View	RI.3.6
2	Vocabulary: Context Clues	L.3.4a
3	Vocabulary: Context Clues	L.3.4a
4	Author's Point of View	RI.3.6
5	Author's Point of View	RI.3.6

Suggested Responses:

1. **Text Evidence:** fun
2. **Text Evidence:** number
3. **Text Evidence:** take good care of
   They help otters that are sick or hurt. They also help pups.
4. The author thinks aquariums help sea otters.
   Text Evidence: The workers help to increase the number of otters in nature.
5. **Text Evidence:** Sea Otters in North America
   to show where sea otters live in North America

UNIT 2 WEEK 5

Item #	Content Focus	CCSS
1	Genre	RL.3.10
2	Literary Elements: Rhyme	RL.2.4
3	Literary Elements: Alliteration	RL.2.4
4	Point of View	RL.3.6
5	Point of View	RL.3.6

Suggested Responses:

1. Each stanza has five lines. The first, second, and fifth lines rhyme. The third and fourth lines rhyme.
2. **Text Evidence:** before, store
   wore
3. **Text Evidence:** whale, wore, was, white
   alliteration
4. **Text Evidence:** The observer just laughed in delight!
5. The poet thinks the events in the poem are funny.

UNIT 3 WEEK 1

Item #	Content Focus	CCSS
1	Problem and Solution	RL.3.1
2	Vocabulary: Context Clues	L.3.4a
3	Problem and Solution	RL.3.1
4	Vocabulary: Context Clues	L.3.4a
5	Problem and Solution	RL.3.1

Suggested Responses:

1. **Text Evidence:** They did not like the way they were made.
2. **Text Evidence:** wonderful
   Fox thinks it would be fabulous if she could run like the wind.
3. They trade legs.
   Text Evidence: Fox and Deer decided to trade legs.
4. **Text Evidence:** different
   Their legs help them in their own ways.
5. **Text Evidence:** Fox and Deer decided to trade again.

UNIT 3 WEEK 2

Item #	Content Focus	CCSS
1	Cause and Effect	RL.3.3
2	Vocabulary: Context Clues	L.3.4a
3	Cause and Effect	RL.3.3
4	Vocabulary: Context Clues	L.3.4a
5	Cause and Effect	RL.3.3

Suggested Responses:

1. He is thinking of his friends.
   Text Evidence: he was thinking of his friends at home
2. **Text Evidence:** never be seen again
   to not be seen; to stop being seen
3. He thinks Tim will be interested in it.
4. **Text Evidence:** surprised
5. He loved nature and wanted to keep it safe.
   Text Evidence: As a result

Weekly Assessment • Answer Key

UNIT 3 WEEK 3

Item #	Content Focus	CCSS
1	Vocabulary: Context Clues	L.3.4a
2	Main Idea and Key Details	RI.3.2
3	Vocabulary: Context Clues	L.3.4a
4	Main Idea and Key Details	RI.3.2
5	Main Idea and Key Details	RI.3.2

Suggested Responses:

1. **Text Evidence:** studied the night sky
   Possible answers: the Sun, planets, moons, stars
2. a planet
   Text Evidence: A moon moves around a planet.
3. **Text Evidence:** The Sun and planets; moons and asteroids
4. more than 90,000
   Text Evidence: 8
5. There are many different objects in our solar system.

UNIT 3 WEEK 4

Item #	Content Focus	CCSS
1	Main Idea and Key Details	RI.3.2
2	Vocabulary: Context Clues	L.3.4a
3	Main Idea and Key Details	RI.3.2
4	Vocabulary: Context Clues	L.3.4a
5	Main Idea and Key Details	RI.3.2

Suggested Responses:

1. They are bone that grows on a buck's head.
   Text Evidence: Antlers are made of bone. They grow on top of the head of a male deer, or buck.
2. **Text Evidence:** different
   the same
3. It shows how antlers look with and without soft covering.
4. **Text Evidence:** looked closely
5. Deer antlers are very strong.
   Text Evidence: Possible answers: Bucks sometimes fight each other with their antlers; Antlers must be tough not to break; They have observed how antlers get strong when they are dry; People want to figure out why antlers are different. This will help them create things as strong as antlers.

UNIT 3 WEEK 5

Item #	Content Focus	CCSS
1	Vocabulary: Context Clues	L.3.4a
2	Sequence	RI.3.3
3	Sequence	RI.3.3
4	Vocabulary: Context Clues	L.3.4a
5	Sequence	RI.3.3

Suggested Responses:

1. **Text Evidence:** went to live in new lands
2. They fought with the natives.
   Text Evidence: Finally
3. bits of old Viking houses
   Text Evidence: Viking tools
4. the first settlers
5. Scandinavia
   Text Evidence: North America

UNIT 4 WEEK 1

Item #	Content Focus	CCSS
1	Vocabulary: Context Clues	L.3.4a
2	Point of View	RL.3.6
3	Vocabulary: Context Clues	L.3.4a
4	Point of View	RL.3.6
5	Point of View	RL.3.6

Suggested Responses:

1. **Text Evidence:** smelling
   a pleasant or nice smell
2. **Text Evidence:** "Is the parrot telling the truth?" I wondered.
   The narrator stops watering the fruit tree.
3. **Text Evidence:** "I was sure he would fly away and find another tree."
4. The narrator is surprised tht the parrot stayed with the tree.
5. The narrator thinks the parrot is a loyal friend. The parrot stayed even though the tree lost the things the parrot loved.

Weekly Assessment • Answer Key

UNIT 4 WEEK 2

Item #	Content Focus	CCSS
1	Vocabulary: Context Clues	L.3.4a
2	Point of View	RL.3.6
3	Point of View	RL.3.6
4	Vocabulary: Context Clues	L.3.4a
5	Point of View	RL.3.6

Suggested Responses:

1. **Text Evidence:** things that we are good at
   natural skills
2. **Text Evidence:** playing music is easier for me than playing sports
3. He thinks he gets better at baseball with his brother's help.
4. **Text Evidence:** closely watched
5. They do different things well.
   Text Evidence: John and I do different things well. I think this makes us a good team.

UNIT 4 WEEK 3

Item #	Content Focus	CCSS
1	Compare and Contrast	RI.3.8
2	Vocabulary: Context Clues	L.3.4a
3	Compare and Contrast	RI.3.8
4	Vocabulary: Context Clues	L.3.4a
5	Compare and Contrast	RI.3.8

Suggested Responses:

1. They have hard shells.
   Text Evidence: Both
2. **Text Evidence:** keep them safe
   something that protects or keeps safe
3. Turtles have webbed feet or long feet to help them swim. Tortoises have thick feet to walk on land.
4. **Text Evidence:** They dig holes in the ground to cover themselves from the heat or cold.
   something that covers or protects
5. [Students may circle any shaded part of the map that shows water and not land.]

UNIT 4 WEEK 4

Item #	Content Focus	CCSS
1	Vocabulary: Context Clues	L.3.4a
2	Cause and Effect	RI.3.3
3	Cause and Effect	RI.3.3
4	Cause and Effect	RI.3.3
5	Vocabulary: Context Clues	L.3.4a

Suggested Responses:

1. to fly
2. People studied flight for hundreds of years.
   Text Evidence: Because of this
3. **Text Evidence:** He was interested in flying.
   So
4. to create thrust
5. **Text Evidence:** we could never fly
   cannot be done

UNIT 4 WEEK 5

Item #	Content Focus	CCSS
1	Genre	RL.3.10
2	Theme	RL.3.2
3	Literary Elements: Rhyme	RL.2.4
4	Literary Elements: Repetition	RL.2.4
5	Theme	RL.3.2

Suggested Responses:

1. The stanzas and lines are not all the same length. Some lines do not rhyme.
2. **Text Evidence:** You show that a great power, / May be found in the smallest flower.
   Even small things can make a difference.
3. **Text Evidence:** light; sight
4. grow
5. Possible answer: The speaker feels happy that the flower is in the woods and wants to help it grow.

Weekly Assessment • Answer Key   Grade 3 **297**

UNIT 5 WEEK 1

Item #	Content Focus	CCSS
1	Vocabulary: Context Clues	L.3.4a
2	Point of View	RL.3.6
3	Point of View	RL.3.6
4	Vocabulary: Context Clues	L.3.4a
5	Point of View	RL.3.6

Suggested Responses:

1. **Text Evidence:** gentle
   In a gentle voice, he says he is hungry and asks for food.
2. **Text Evidence:** The older brother had bread, but he did not want to give it away. So, he told the old man to go away.
3. He feels sorry for the man.
   Text Evidence: This brother felt bad for him and gave his lunch away for free.
4. **Text Evidence:** a goose with feathers made of pure gold
   something used to pay for something else
5. He is happy and excited about his gift.
   Text Evidence: Now his family could afford wood and more!

UNIT 5 WEEK 2

Item #	Content Focus	CCSS
1	Vocabulary: Context Clues	L.3.4a
2	Point of View	RL.3.6
3	Point of View	RL.3.6
4	Vocabulary: Context Clues	L.3.4a
5	Point of View	RL.3.6

Suggested Responses:

1. **Text Evidence:** because it was raining and he could not play outside
   a state of being upset because you cannot do something
2. **Text Evidence:** Tina knew her brother loved pirates.
3. He thinks it is important that pirates have a treasure map.
   Text Evidence: Mark thought the most important thing pirates needed was a treasure map.
4. **Text Evidence:** very happy
5. They think that making what they needed was as much fun as playing pirates.
   Text Evidence: They thought it had been just as much fun making what they needed as it was to actually play.

UNIT 5 WEEK 3

Item #	Content Focus	CCSS
1	Author's Point of View	RI.3.6
2	Vocabulary: Context Clues	L.3.4a
3	Author's Point of View	RI.3.6
4	Vocabulary: Context Clues	L.3.4a
5	Author's Point of View	RI.3.6

Suggested Responses:

1. **Text Evidence:** People watch the news to learn about events in their community. The news tells people what is happening around them.
2. It reacts quickly to events.
3. **Text Evidence:** Reporting the news on TV takes amazing teamwork.
4. **Text Evidence:** tools
5. Their job is like the job of a host on TV.
   Text Evidence: News anchors are like the hosts of the news program.

UNIT 5 WEEK 4

Item #	Content Focus	CCSS
1	Vocabulary: Context Clues	L.3.4a
2	Author's Point of View	RI.3.6
3	Vocabulary: Context Clues	L.3.4a
4	Author's Point of View	RI.3.6
5	Author's Point of View	RI.3.6

Suggested Responses:

1. **Text Evidence:** The people lived hard lives while others lived in comfort.
   not fair or just
2. She taught workers how to live their lives better and healthier. She also reported unsafe workplaces.
3. **Text Evidence:** She did many more things to help others
4. **Text Evidence:** 1902 Becomes a teacher at a settlement house for workers; 1903 Reports on workplaces for the Consumer's League
5. Possible answer: The author thinks Eleanor worked hard so that people could have better lives and our country could be a better place to live.
   Text Evidence: As First Lady, Eleanor continued working to improve people's lives. She did many more things to help others and make our country a better place.

Weekly Assessment · Answer Key

UNIT 5 WEEK 5

Item #	Content Focus	CCSS
1	Vocabulary: Context Clues	L.3.4a
2	Cause and Effect	RI.3.3
3	Vocabulary: Context Clues	L.3.4a
4	Cause and Effect	RI.3.3
5	Cause and Effect	RI.3.3

Suggested Responses:

1. **Text Evidence:** power
   the ability to do work
2. The blades turn.
   Text Evidence: causes
3. **Text Evidence:** will not run out
4. Wind power will not run out or pollute the earth.
   Text Evidence: As a result
5. Coal and Oil

UNIT 6 WEEK 1

Item #	Content Focus	CCSS
1	Vocabulary: Context Clues	L.3.4a
2	Theme	RL.3.2
3	Vocabulary: Context Clues	L.3.4a
4	Theme	RL.3.2
5	Theme	RL.3.2

Suggested Responses:

1. fire
   Text Evidence: They should have it
2. **Text Evidence:** No! Humans would become too strong with fire.
   Humans would become strong like the gods.
3. **Text Evidence:** pain
4. **Text Evidence:** *Prometheus steals fire at Zeus's home and brings it to Elana.*
5. It is more important to do what is right than to please your friends.
   Text Evidence: But it was the right thing to do.

UNIT 6 WEEK 2

Item #	Content Focus	CCSS
1	Theme	RL.3.2
2	Vocabulary: Context Clues	L.3.4a
3	Vocabulary: Context Clues	L.3.4a
4	Theme	RL.3.2
5	Theme	RL.3.2

Suggested Responses:

1. Her son is sick and needs water.
   Text Evidence: Abby's son, Henry, had a fever and needed fresh water badly.
2. **Text Evidence:** leave him
   to be left in a helpless position
3. **Text Evidence:** On her way home, Abby saw people holding ice to their skin to cool off.
   freedom from discomfort or pain
4. **Text Evidence:** She had been away for hours. What if his fever had gotten worse? . . . Henry needed the ice more than she did.
5. We should think of others before we think of ourselves.

UNIT 6 WEEK 3

Item #	Content Focus	CCSS
1	Vocabulary: Context Clues	L.3.4a
2	Problem and Solution	RI.3.3
3	Problem and Solution	RI.3.3
4	Problem and Solution	RI.3.3
5	Vocabulary: Context Clues	L.3.4a

Suggested Responses:

1. **Text Evidence:** Mae C. Jemison planned to travel to outer space.
   something that someone wants to do
2. **Text Evidence:** some people told her not to study math and science in college
3. She studied math, science, and other subjects.
4. **Text Evidence:** the care that doctors give people to help them get and stay healthy
   She became a leader and role model for other medical workers. She also tried to keep people healthy.
5. **Text Evidence:** tried to find ways
   studies to learn more about something

Weekly Assessment • Answer Key   Grade 3   301

UNIT 6 WEEK 4

Item #	Content Focus	CCSS
1	Vocabulary: Context Clues	L.3.4a
2	Compare and Contrast	RI.3.8
3	Vocabulary: Context Clues	L.3.4a
4	Compare and Contrast	RI.3.8
5	Compare and Contrast	RI.3.7

Suggested Responses:

1. **Text Evidence:** live
2. **Text Evidence:** All whales are mammals
   The narwhal is the only whale that has a long tusk.
3. **Text Evidence:** Scientists want to learn more about it.
   very interesting
4. The narwhal uses its tusk to compete for females.
5. blow hole, fins, and tail

UNIT 6 WEEK 5

Item #	Content Focus	CCSS
1	Point of View	RL.3.6
2	Literary Elements: Rhyme	RL.2.4
3	Literary Elements: Rhythm	RL.2.4
4	Point of View	RL.3.6
5	Genre	RL.3.10

Suggested Responses:

1. The narrator likes the tree and wants to sit under it.
   Text Evidence: The song was sweet and made me smile. / I said, "Why, I'll just sit awhile."
2. **Text Evidence:** sway
   rhyme
3. **Text Evidence:** took; out; had; look
   rhythm
4. It is no longer fun to sit under the tree.
5. The tree is dropping nuts, so the narrator runs away.

Mid-Unit Assessment Answer Key

UNIT 1

Item #	Answer	Content Focus	CCSS
1	B	Character	RL.3.3
2	C	Vocabulary: Context Clues	L.3.4a
3	C	Sequence	RL.3.3
4	A	Sequence	RL.3.3
5	B	Character	RL.3.3
6	C	Vocabulary: Context Clues	L.3.4a
7	B	Sequence	RI.3.3
8	A	Sequence	RI.3.3
9	C	Vocabulary: Context Clues	L.3.4a
10	B	Sequence	RI.3.3

Mid-Unit Assessment • Answer Key

UNIT 2

Item #	Answer	Content Focus	CCSS
1	C	Theme	RL.3.2
2	A	Theme	RL.3.2
3	B	Vocabulary: Context Clues	L.3.4a
4	C	Theme	RL.3.2
5	A	Vocabulary: Context Clues	L.3.4a
6	C	Author's Point of View	RI.3.6
7	B	Author's Point of View	RI.3.6
8	C	Vocabulary: Context Clues	L.3.4a
9	A	Author's Point of View	RI.3.6
10	A	Text Features: Bar Graph	RI.3.7

UNIT 3

Item #	Answer	Content Focus	CCSS
1	B	Problem and Solution	RL.3.1
2	B	Cause and Effect	RL.3.3
3	A	Cause and Effect	RL.3.3
4	C	Vocabulary: Context Clues	L.3.4a
5	A	Problem and Solution	RL.3.1
6	B	Main Idea and Key Details	RI.3.2
7	C	Vocabulary: Context Clues	L.3.4a
8	B	Main Idea and Key Details	RI.3.2
9	C	Vocabulary: Context Clues	L.3.4a
10	A	Text Features: Charts	RI.3.5

Mid-Unit Assessment • Answer Key

UNIT 4

Item #	Answer	Content Focus	CCSS
1	A	Point of View	RL.3.6
2	B	Point of View	RL.3.6
3	C	Vocabulary: Context Clues	L.3.4a
4	A	Vocabulary: Context Clues	L.3.4a
5	C	Point of View	RL.3.6
6	C	Compare and Contrast	RI.3.8
7	B	Compare and Contrast	RI.3.8
8	C	Text Features: Map	RI.3.7
9	B	Vocabulary: Context Clues	L.3.4a
10	A	Compare and Contrast	RI.3.8

UNIT 5

Item #	Answer	Content Focus	CCSS
1	C	Point of View	RL.3.6
2	A	Point of View	RL.3.6
3	A	Vocabulary: Context Clues	L.3.4a
4	C	Vocabulary: Context Clues	L.3.4a
5	C	Point of View	RL.3.6
6	B	Vocabulary: Context Clues	L.3.4a
7	A	Author's Point of View	RI.3.6
8	C	Author's Point of View	RI.3.6
9	B	Text Features: Headings	RI.3.5
10	C	Author's Point of View	RI.3.6

Mid-Unit Assessment • Answer Key

UNIT 6

Item #	Answer	Content Focus	CCSS
1	B	Vocabulary: Context Clues	L.3.4a
2	B	Vocabulary: Context Clues	L.3.4a
3	A	Theme	RL.3.2
4	C	Theme	RL.3.2
5	C	Theme	RL.3.2
6	A	Problem and Solution	RI.3.3
7	C	Text Features: Keywords	RI.3.5
8	C	Vocabulary: Context Clues	L.3.4a
9	A	Problem and Solution	RI.3.3
10	C	Problem and Solution	RI.3.3

Unit Assessment Answer Key

UNIT 1

Item #	Answer	Content Focus	CCSS
1	C	Character	RL.3.3
2	B	Vocabulary: Context Clues	L.3.4a
3	A	Sequence	RL.3.3
4	B	Character	RL.3.3
5	C	Character	RL.3.3
6	A	Vocabulary: Context Clues	L.3.4a
7	B	Sequence	RL.3.3
8	A	Vocabulary: Context Clues	L.3.4a
9	C	Sequence	RI.3.3
10	B	Main Idea and Key Details	RI.3.2
11	B	Vocabulary: Context Clues	L.3.4a
12	A	Cause and Effect	RI.3.3
13	B	Vocabulary: Context Clues	L.3.4a
14	C	Main Idea and Key Details	RI.3.2
15	C	Text Features: Map	RI.3.7

UNIT 2

Item #	Answer	Content Focus	CCSS
1	C	Point of View	RL.3.6
2	A	Theme	RL.3.2
3	C	Vocabulary: Context Clues	L.3.4a
4	C	Theme	RL.3.2
5	B	Vocabulary: Context Clues	L.3.4a
6	C	Point of View	RL.3.6
7	B	Vocabulary: Context Clues	L.3.4a
8	A	Theme	RL.3.2
9	A	Vocabulary: Context Clues	L.3.4a
10	B	Author's Point of View	RI.3.6
11	B	Author's Point of View	RI.3.6
12	C	Text Features: Map	RI.3.7
13	A	Vocabulary: Context Clues	L.3.4a
14	C	Author's Point of View	RI.3.6
15	B	Author's Point of View	RI.3.6

UNIT 3

Item #	Answer	Content Focus	CCSS
1	B	Cause and Effect	RL.3.3
2	A	Problem and Solution	RL.3.1
3	B	Problem and Solution	RL.3.1
4	A	Vocabulary: Context Clues	L.3.4a
5	B	Cause and Effect	RL.3.3
6	C	Vocabulary: Context Clues	L.3.4a
7	C	Problem and Solution	RL.3.1
8	A	Main Idea and Key Details	RI.3.2
9	C	Sequence	RI.3.3
10	A	Vocabulary: Context Clues	L.3.4a
11	B	Sequence	RI.3.3
12	C	Vocabulary: Context Clues	L.3.4a
13	B	Text Features: Chart	RI.3.5
14	A	Vocabulary: Context Clues	L.3.4a
15	C	Main Idea and Key Details	RI.3.2

Unit Assessment · Answer Key

UNIT 4

Item #	Answer	Content Focus	CCSS
1	C	Point of View	RL.3.6
2	B	Point of View	RL.3.6
3	B	Vocabulary: Context Clues	L.3.4a
4	C	Vocabulary: Context Clues	L.3.4a
5	A	Point of View	RL.3.6
6	B	Vocabulary: Context Clues	L.3.4a
7	A	Theme	RL.3.2
8	C	Theme	RL.3.2
9	A	Vocabulary: Context Clues	L.3.4a
10	A	Compare and Contrast	RI.3.8
11	B	Compare and Contrast	RI.3.8
12	A	Cause and Effect	RI.3.3
13	C	Cause and Effect	RI.3.3
14	A	Compare and Contrast	RI.3.8
15	C	Vocabulary: Context Clues	L.3.4a

UNIT 5

Item #	Answer	Content Focus	CCSS
1	B	Point of View	RL.3.6
2	A	Point of View	RL.3.6
3	B	Vocabulary: Context Clues	L.3.4a
4	A	Point of View	RL.3.6
5	B	Vocabulary: Context Clues	L.3.4a
6	C	Vocabulary: Context Clues	L.3.4a
7	A	Point of View	RL.3.6
8	C	Point of View	RL.3.6
9	A	Vocabulary: Context Clues	L.3.4a
10	A	Author's Point of View	RI.3.6
11	C	Cause and Effect	RI.3.3
12	B	Vocabulary: Context Clues	L.3.4a
13	C	Cause and Effect	RI.3.3
14	C	Author's Point of View	RI.3.6
15	A	Text Features: Chart	RI.3.5

Unit Assessment • Answer Key

UNIT 6

Item #	Answer	Content Focus	CCSS
1	A	Point of View	RL.3.6
2	C	Vocabulary: Context Clues	L.3.4a
3	C	Vocabulary: Context Clues	L.3.4a
4	B	Point of View	RL.3.6
5	A	Theme	RL.3.2
6	B	Vocabulary: Context Clues	L.3.4a
7	C	Theme	RL.3.2
8	A	Compare and Contrast	RI.3.8
9	A	Vocabulary: Context Clues	L.3.4a
10	C	Compare and Contrast	RI.3.8
11	A	Compare and Contrast	RI.3.8
12	A	Problem and Solution	RI.3.3
13	C	Vocabulary: Context Clues	L.3.4a
14	B	Problem and Solution	RI.3.3
15	B	Text Features: Diagram	RI.3.7

Exit Assessment Answer Key

UNIT 1

Item #	Answer	Content Focus	CCSS
1	B	Vocabulary: Context Clues	L.3.4a
2	C	Character	RL.3.3
3	A	Vocabulary: Context Clues	L.3.4a
4	B	Sequence	RL.3.3
5	A	Sequence	RL.3.3
6	B	Character	RL.3.3
7	C	Vocabulary: Context Clues	L.3.4a
8	C	Character	RL.3.3
9	B	Sequence	RI.3.3
10	C	Vocabulary: Context Clues	L.3.4a
11	B	Main Idea and Key Details	RI.3.2
12	A	Main Idea and Key Details	RI.3.2
13	B	Vocabulary: Context Clues	L.3.4a
14	A	Cause and Effect	RI.3.3
15	B	Text Features: Diagram	RI.3.7

Exit Assessment · Answer Key

UNIT 2

Item #	Answer	Content Focus	CCSS
1	A	Vocabulary: Context Clues	L.3.4a
2	B	Theme	RL.3.2
3	A	Point of View	RL.3.6
4	C	Vocabulary: Context Clues	L.3.4a
5	A	Point of View	RL.3.6
6	C	Vocabulary: Context Clues	L.3.4a
7	B	Point of View	RL.3.6
8	B	Theme	RL.3.2
9	C	Vocabulary: Context Clues	L.3.4a
10	A	Author's Point of View	RI.3.6
11	B	Vocabulary: Context Clues	L.3.4a
12	C	Author's Point of View	RI.3.6
13	A	Author's Point of View	RI.3.6
14	B	Author's Point of View	RI.3.6
15	C	Text Features: Bar Graph	RI.3.7

UNIT 3

Item #	Answer	Content Focus	CCSS
1	C	Vocabulary: Context Clues	L.3.4a
2	A	Problem and Solution	RL.3.1
3	C	Vocabulary: Context Clues	L.3.4a
4	A	Cause and Effect	RL.3.3
5	C	Problem and Solution	RL.3.1
6	B	Cause and Effect	RL.3.3
7	B	Vocabulary: Context Clues	L.3.4a
8	A	Cause and Effect	RL.3.3
9	C	Vocabulary: Context Clues	L.3.4a
10	C	Sequence	RI.3.3
11	A	Main Idea and Key Details	RI.3.2
12	B	Sequence	RI.3.3
13	C	Vocabulary: Context Clues	L.3.4a
14	B	Main Idea and Key Details	RI.3.2
15	A	Text Features: Chart	RI.3.5

Exit Assessment • Answer Key

UNIT 4

Item #	Answer	Content Focus	CCSS
1	A	Point of View	RL.3.6
2	C	Point of View	RL.3.6
3	A	Vocabulary: Context Clues	L.3.4a
4	B	Theme	RL.3.2
5	A	Vocabulary: Context Clues	L.3.4a
6	C	Point of View	RL.3.6
7	B	Vocabulary: Context Clues	L.3.4a
8	B	Theme	RL.3.2
9	A	Cause and Effect	RI.3.3
10	C	Compare and Contrast	RI.3.8
11	B	Vocabulary: Context Clues	L.3.4a
12	C	Cause and Effect	RI.3.3
13	B	Vocabulary: Context Clues	L.3.4a
14	A	Compare and Contrast	RI.3.8
15	A	Cause and Effect	RI.3.3

UNIT 5

Item #	Answer	Content Focus	CCSS
1	A	Point of View	RL.3.6
2	A	Vocabulary: Context Clues	L.3.4a
3	C	Point of View	RL.3.6
4	B	Point of View	RL.3.6
5	A	Point of View	RL.3.6
6	B	Vocabulary: Context Clues	L.3.4a
7	B	Vocabulary: Context Clues	L.3.4a
8	A	Point of View	RL.3.6
9	A	Author's Point of View	RI.3.6
10	C	Vocabulary: Context Clues	L.3.4a
11	A	Cause and Effect	RI.3.3
12	C	Vocabulary: Context Clues	L.3.4a
13	C	Cause and Effect	RI.3.3
14	A	Author's Point of View	RI.3.6
15	A	Text Features: Time Line	RI.3.7

Exit Assessment • Answer Key   Grade 3   **319**

UNIT 6

Item #	Answer	Content Focus	CCSS
1	A	Point of View	RL.3.6
2	A	Vocabulary: Context Clues	L.3.4a
3	B	Point of View	RL.3.6
4	B	Vocabulary: Context Clues	L.3.4a
5	A	Vocabulary: Context Clues	L.3.4a
6	C	Theme	RL.3.2
7	C	Theme	RL.3.2
8	B	Text Features: Keywords	RI.3.5
9	A	Vocabulary: Context Clues	L.3.4a
10	B	Problem and Solution	RI.3.3
11	C	Problem and Solution	RI.3.3
12	A	Compare and Contrast	RI.3.8
13	B	Compare and Contrast	RI.3.8
14	C	Compare and Contrast	RI.3.8
15	A	Vocabulary: Context Clues	L.3.4a